Contents

A History of Hot Air and Caloric Engines

A History of
Hot Air
and Caloric
Engines

Robert Sier

ARGUS BOOKS

Argus Books Ltd
1 Golden Square
London W1R 3AB
England

ISBN 0 85242 900 2

Phototypesetting by Photocomp Ltd., Birmingham

Printed and bound by Richard Clay Ltd., Bungay, Suffolk

Preface

The research that led to writing this book was started when, having built a small hot air engine to the words and music of a book which was intended I think for school metalwork classes, I found that the building was one thing but making the wheels go round was another. There was, at that time, little information on the subject readily available on the shelves of the local library, although several books on modern developments have since been published.

The *Model Engineer* now holds an annual Hot Air Engine competition, which has also stimulated much interest in the subject of small hot air engines. Although much has been written on the history and development of the steam engine and the internal combustion engine, there is still little information on the early history of the mechanical use of heated air where heat is derived from either external or internal non-explosive combustion, a gap I hope this book will bridge.

I would like to thank the staff of Romford and Chelmsford Libraries for obtaining many books for me over the past few years and the staff of the Science Museum and Patent Office libraries for their help in unearthing information, and also to a well-known broadcasting company, for without their microcomputer I never would have finished. Finally, I am grateful to my wife without whose encouragement I never would have started and who has tolerated many years of Hot Air Engines dominating the household.

Chelmsford 1986   R. Sier

Opposite, **Plate 1**   Heinrici motor

Plate 2 Howard engine

Introduction

The methods used in obtaining power from heated air are many and varied, ranging from displacing fluids in overbalancing wheels and acting on pistons in hot air engines to using the increased buoyancy of heated air to drive round fans or fly hot air balloons.

Who invented the hot air engine is something I leave the reader to decide. It is interesting to compare the different paths taken by the three early pioneers in the field of piston driven air engines: Cayley, Stirling, and Ericsson.

George Cayley, who probably made the first attempt at constructing a working engine, was looking for a suitable alternative to the steam engine in providing motive power to aerial and road transport. Cayley's design, however, proved to be only suitable for stationary engine working, although it could be claimed that with the perfecting of the gas turbine Cayley's basic design now powers the world's airways.

Robert Stirling designs looked for economy in fuel consumption, with his ideas translated into actual engines by his brother James who constructed large machines from beam engine parts. Although displacer type machines were built in large numbers, Stirling's regenerator was rarely used and only with the recent development work of the Philips Company has the regenerator returned to form a vital part of the modern hot gas engine. The Philips machine can truly be called a 'Stirling Engine' while the old displacer engines are best called, as they always were, Hot Air Engines. John Ericsson's second patent was for a ship's engine, to replace steam, something he never achieved with his caloric ships. Ericsson was the only one to have built his engines on a commercial basis for profit, and seems to have made a great deal of money from them. His caloric engine was not taken up by other designers to any extent, and his experiments in solar power caused him to turn to the displacer engine, which, while not realising his expectations of power from the sun, was successfully sold in large numbers, powered by other sources of heat.

The use of hot air engines diminished with the advent of electric power and development of the internal combustion engine: the greatest use was in the field of water pumping, with engines being sold up to the late 1920s. Another use was for driving ventilating fans, and the production of these machines is still carried on in Pakistan.

The present rebirth of the air engine is due entirely to the development work carried out by the Philips Research Laboratory in Eindhoven, Holland. Philips originally turned to the hot air engine, during the 1930s, in a search for a suitable power supply to enable the use of Philips radio sets in areas of the world without electricity. However, the development of the transistor and improvements in the dry cell meant that radios could be used independent of a regular electrical supply, and this led to the discontinuation of production of generating sets in 1954, after some 100 sets had been built, for want of a suitable market. Philips, however, did not stop research into Stirling engines, switching to the development of engines with larger power outputs, up to hundreds of horse power, instead. The Philips engine has also been taken up by General Motors and Ford for development as a vehicle engine.

The volume of literature on the modern air engine is large and ever-increasing. A good bibliography is to be found in Graham Walker's book *Stirling Engines* which covers every aspect of designing the modern hot gas or Stirling engine, and for the model engineer there is James Rizzo's book *Modelling Stirling and Hot Air Engines*.

2

The water displacement engine

There is regrettably little written material available on the use of heat for the generating of power before the sixteenth century. One can only speculate as to the number of books that have been lost through fire, wars, natural disasters or the actions of religious fanatics. What we do have are scraps written in Greek, Latin, Arabic and Chinese. From this information it is clear that much scientific work was accomplished in the four centuries before Christ, though with the passing of time one cannot with any certainty give individual credit for original ideas. Most credit has come to be associated with those in whose writings they appear. It is in the works of the Greeks of the Hellenestic age that the first references to mechanics are to be found; we know little of early science or engineering in Iran, India or China, as the written word has long since perished.

The first known reference to what we now call the 'spring of air' is found in the works of Straton. Straton lived in the third century BC and was a student of Aristotle; his works have survived only as fragments quoted by later authors. Unlike Aristotle he accepted atoms, explaining that a vacuum was the space between atoms. In air this space decreased when the air was compressed, forcing closer together the atoms, and increased when air was rarefied.

Possibly the earliest known reference to the expansion of air by means of heat is found in the works of Philo of Byzantium, who lived possibly during the second century BC or earlier. Only a small proportion of his works has survived, but among it is his *De ingeniis spiritualibus*. The Greek original is lost although an Arabic and a Latin copy survive. In this work he describes the following instrument for demonstrating that air expands on heating:

A hollow leaden globe of moderate size is made . . . the interior of which should be quite dry. Through a hole in the top, a tube is fitted, one end of which passes down nearly to the bottom of the globe, and the other end is bent over and placed in a vessel filled with water (also reaching to the bottom) . . . I assert that when the globe is placed in the sun and becomes warm, some of the air enclosed in the tube will pass out. This will be seen since the air flows out of the tube into the water, setting it in motion and producing air bubbles, one after the other. If the globe be placed in the shade, or any other place where the sun does not penetrate, the water will rise through the tube and flow into the globe . . . As often as this process is repeated, the same result occurs. If the globe be heated with fire, or hot water be poured on it, the same effect is produced. On cooling the globe, the water again rises.

The first examples of air engines that we have appear in the works of Heron of Alexandria, written possibly in the first century AD (1). In his works Heron describes mechanisms originated by himself and also others invented by other authors, but unfortunately at no time does he indicate the origin of each invention, so we cannot be sure of the period when each device was conceived. Written in an age where the water wheel and animal power were quite able to meet the power requirements for pumping water and grinding flour, the devices described are perhaps more for amusement and to impress the unscientific rather than as potential sources of power.

The only heat engine to have been used in Greek and Roman times was a steam blower for fires. Vitruvius writing in the first century AD gave the following description:

. . . Now figures of Aeolus are made of hollow bronze and they have a very narrow point, they are filled with water and placed on the fire; before they begin to warm, they have no rush of air, but as soon as they begin to boil they produce on the fire a vehement blast.

These blowers inspired the whirling steam engine described by Heron. An air-operated version was also described for making figures dance when a fire was placed upon an altar. The altar was constructed of glass or horn to be transparent (fig. 1.1). A tube was let down from the altar, the top attached to the altar and the bottom turning on a pivot. Four tubes are connected as shown and fastened to these is a platform on which figures stand. When the fire was lit the air became heated and expanded through the bent pipes and when meeting resistance (from the sides) caused the platform to rotate.

4

Fig. 1.1 Heron, dancing figures

All the other devices described by Heron work by displacing fluid by means of air expanded by heat.

In two examples libations are offered when a fire is lit upon an altar. In fig. 1.2 the heated air presses onto the surface of wine, stored in the bottom of the pedestal, so forcing the wine up through the tubes along the figures' arms and so onto the fire. The altar is connected to the pedestal by a pipe which Heron states 'should be broader towards the middle, for it is requisite that the heat, or rather the vapour from it, passing into a broader space should expand and act with greater force'. In fig. 1.3 the wine is contained in vessels within the bodies of the figures, but is displaced as before. Three tubes come from the altar, one

Fig. 1.2 Heron, figures offering libations

5

Fig. 1.3 Heron, figures offering libations

Fig. 1.4 Heron, solar fountain

to each figure and the third to the snake, the hot air passing out of its mouth to make a hissing sound. In this case Heron states that a little water should first be poured into the tubes so that they may not be burnt by the dry heat. The hot air and water pass along the tubes to act on the wine. These two examples form propositions eleven and sixty in Heron's treatise and he makes no attempt to compare them.

Along similar lines 'A fountain which trickles by the action of the sun rays' is described. A globe is half filled with water with an air space as shown in fig. 1.4. When the sun's rays heat up the globe, the enclosed air expands, displacing the air out through the siphon G, passing through the funnel into the pedestal. When the globe is placed in the shade the air cools and so sucks up water from the pedestal.

6

Water displacement is also proposed for opening temple doors (fig. 1.5). An airtight altar is connected to a globe which is filled with water. The heat of the fire expands the air in the altar which then acts on water in the globe, displacing it via the siphon into the bucket. The mechanism for opening the door consists of chains wrapped around the door pivots, with a leaden counterweight keeping the door shut. When water fills the bucket the counterbalance is overcome and the doors open. When the fire is extinguished the air will cool, so sucking back the water into the globe, and the counterbalance then closes the door. Heron states that 'some in place of water use quicksilver, as it is heavier than water and easily disunited by fire'.

An alternative method for opening doors is shown in fig. 1.6. Here two weights are used in conjunction with a leather bag. The pressure of the heated air expands the bag, so lifting the weight L, allowing the counterweight B to open the doors. When the fire is extinguished the weight will fall, closing the doors. It is necessary for the weight L to be the heavier; the bag is initially folded together. The weight B was optional as Heron states 'The doors will either open of themselves, as the doors of baths shut spontaneously, or they may have a counterbalance weight to open them'.

This method of opening the temple doors was probably derived from the water clock. Vitruvius decribes the making of a water clock called Anaphorica (book IX C VII):

Fig. 1.5 Heron, opening temple doors

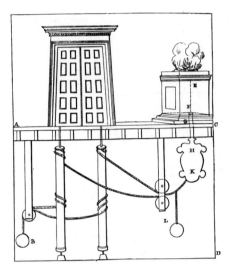

Fig. 1.6 Heron, opening temple doors

On the axle a pliable brass chain is coiled. On one end hangs a cork or drum raised by the water; on the other, a counter poise of sand equal in weight to the cork. Thus so far as the cork is raised by the water to that extent the weight of the sand drags down and turns the axle.

In his chapter on temples and temple doors Vitruvius makes no mention of these mechanisms for opening or closing doors. In Greek and Roman temples the altar was outside the temple in the precinct, so it may have been possible for a priest to have operated the mechanism.

Vitruvius tells us that the 'altar should look to the east and always be placed lower than the images which shall be in the temple so that those who pray and sacrifice may look up to the divinity from various levels as becomes each man's god.' The use of fire on altars went back many centuries, and the following is taken from the 2nd book of Kings ch 16:

> And king Ahaz went to Damascus to meet Tiglath-pilser, king of Assyria, and saw an altar that was at Damascus: and king Ahaz sent to Urijah the priest the fashion of the altar, and the pattern of it, according to all the workmanship thereof. And Urizah the priest built an altar according to all that king Ahaz had sent from Damascus: so Urijah the priest made it against king Ahaz came from Damascus. And when the king was come from Damascus, the king saw the altar: and the king approached the altar, and offered thereon. And he burnt his

burnt offering and his meat offering, and poured his drink offering, and sprinkled the blood of his peace offerings, upon the altar.

And he brought also the brazen altar, which was before the LORD, from the front of the house, from between the altar and the house of the lord, and put it on the north side of the altar. And king Ahaz commanded Urijah the priest, saying, 'Upon the great altar burn the morning burnt offering, and the evening meat offering, and the king's burnt sacrifice, and his meat offering, with the burnt offering of all the people of the land, and their meat offering, and all the blood of the sacrifice; and the brazen altar shall be for me to enquire by.' Thus did Urijah the priest, according to all that king Ahaz commanded.

King Ahaz was the 11th king of Judah and reigned in the 7th century BC, i.e. 700 years before Heron and Vitruvius.

Little is known of any use of the mechanical properties of heat until the reappearance of Heron's work in the sixteenth century. A Latin version appeared in 1573 as his *Spiritalia at Urbino*, and this was followed by two editions, printed in Italian, published in 1589. One translated by Battesta Allcotti d'Argenta and published at Ferrara gave descriptions and woodcuts of Heron's heat engines, the illustrations being identical to those of the Latin edition of 1573.

One possible outcome of this reprinting was the Air-Thermoscope. The term thermoscope is used here to describe a class of thermometer that gives an indication of temperature change rather than a measure of temperature. The first instrument may have been made by Galileo and consisted of a long glass tube open at one end with a glass bulb at the other. The glass tube was filled with water, the level of the water giving the visual indication of temperature change. To fill the tube with water the glass bulb was first heated, the open end then placed in a vessel containing water. As the air cooled the water was sucked up the tube and any subsequent change in the temperature of the air in the bulb was indicated by the level of the water rising or falling.

An early example of a thermoscope is to be found in a manuscript entitled *Mathematica maravigliosa*, written in 1611 by Bartolomeo Teoioux. The apparatus consisted of two flasks with necks at least one foot in length, the diameter of the necks being such that the neck of one flask could be inserted into the other. Before this was done the lower flask was filled to about three-quarters of its capacity with water. The scale comprised eight degrees and was numbered up the neck of the larger vessel on both sides, and each degree was further subdivided into six parts (6).

One of the first applications was to medical problems and an example is found in the works of Santorio Santorrii (1561-1636), a professor of medicine in Padua (14). His thermoscope (fig. 1.7) consisted of a long tube with a bulb at one end, the lower end being encased for approximately one sixth of its length by a cylindrical vessel containing the indicating liquid. There was a small hole in the wall of this vessel near the top where it was sealed to the tube. Santorrii used his device to measure the heat of a patient's heart by measuring the heat of expelled air, which was supposed to come from the heart. With the patient holding the bulb in his hands or with it placed in his mouth, Santorrii observed the distance that the liquid moved during ten beats of a small pendulum. As this depended on not only the patient's temperature but also the speed of his peripheral circulation, which increases with fever, this method was probably a good indication of fever. A similar apparatus was used by Robert Fludd (in 1617) to demonstrate, he claimed, the cosmic effects of light and darkness and heat and cold, to indicate or predict weather conditions, and to measure temperature changes (15).

The air thermometer was used for various functions though mainly for medical purposes, but was very inaccurate and particularly sensitive to changes in atmospheric pressure, which led to the development of the closed type of thermometer.

A popular form of thermoscope was the Weather Glass, also known as a water barometer, old Dutch weather glass, Liege barometer or calendar glass.

An early description, given in 1634 by John Bate, of a weather glass describes it as a:

> Structure of at least two glasses (a tube and the vessel containing the water) sometimes three, four, or more on accasion serveth, inclosing a quantity of water and a proporcionable: by whose condensacion downard; by which mocion of the water is commonly forshown the state, change and alteracion of the weather; for I speak no more than what my own experieance hath made me bold to affirm; you may (the time of the year, and the following observation understandingly considered) be able to fortell the alteracion or uncertainty of the weather a good many hours before it comes to pass! (7).

The following is taken from an engraving, dated 1631, entitled:

> *A Table Plainly Teaching Ye Making and Use of a Wether Glass.* Prepare 2 glasse like into these figures marked with AAA and EE then into ye mouth of EE fit a close cork through which make a hole

10

Fig. 1.7 Santorrii, Thermoscope (c1600)

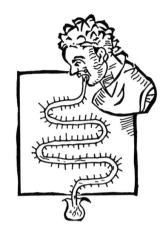

through it put ye shank of AAA & fasten it so that so that it being put into glas EE may rech almost into ye botom divide the space beetween bodie of AAA & the cork so fastened into 16 eqall pts next fil ye glas EE almost as full as ye can of fair water warened if ye hath some Roman vitrol disolved in it the heate ye head of AAA verie well at ye fier and put it into ye glas EE & wax it fast & you shall peceive the water to ascend into it beehould ye fugure BBB lastly include EE in a box as bb.

THE USE
1. Note ye this water ascendeth with could & desceneth with heate
2. If in 6 or 8 hower ye water fale a degree or more it will sureli rain within 12 hours after
3. so long as ye water stands at any one degre so long ye wether wil continue at ye stay it is the at
lastly by diligent Observac ye may fortel frost snow or feol wether
You may bye the glasses aaa & ee at the signe of the Princes Leaden Hale Street.

Several large examples of weather glasses were built in the seventeenth century.

Otto Guerick (1602-82), mayor of Magdeburg, Germany, had made in about 1660 a large air thermometer, some 10 feet tall, constructed of copper and brass. It was suspended from an outside wall of his house. The working fluid was spirits of wine, to prevent freezing during the winter months, set in a U tube. The level was indicated by a cork that floated upon a liquid and to which was attached cord that ran over a

11

pulley to a suspended pointer in the form of an angel. Guerick made the device in order to find the coolest and the warmest days of the year.

Otto Guerick is probably better known for his air pump with which he demonstrated the power of vacuum (16).

Richard Townley of Townley Hall, Lancashire, erected in 1661 a similar device against an outer wall, constructed of lead piping in the form of a J with the shortest limb taken into the basement where a float indicated changes in water level. The experiment was not a success as the results were too dependent on temperature and air pressure, and the device was dismantled in favour of a mercury barometer (17).

Dutch weather glasses or air thermometers took the form of a J shaped tube with a closed bulb at the top of the long leg and an open bulb at the mouth of the short leg; they possibly came into general use by 1625 at the latest. Their origin is not certain though the invention has been ascribed to Cornelius Drebble (1572-1633) of Alkamaar, Holland. Liege barometers took the form of a glass vessel shaped like a pear cut in half and fitted with a spout like a coffee pot.

The weather glass indicates changes in temperature as well as pressure but provided it is kept in that part of the house where there is a reasonably constant temperature it does give a reasonably adequate indication of changes in weather. As late as 1897 a patent was taken out for improvements in weather glasses and weather glasses were sold in Britain up to 1939.

The publication of Heron's works also kindled interest in the raising of water by means of heat.

In 1608 Porta (1538-1615) described a method of raising water (3). A closed vessel of brass was to be placed upon a tower, having a pipe

Fig. 1.8 Porta, raising water (1608)

12

connected to its open part and extending down to the water to be raised, the orifice being a short distance below the surface. The vessel was then to be made hot by the sun or by 'fire' to rarefy the contained air and expel a portion of it through the pipe. As the vessel grows cold, he observed, the remaining air is condensed, and because it cannot then fill the vacuity the 'water is called in and ascends thither' (fig. 1.8).

The same idea of raising water by the sun's rays appears in the works of de Caus (1615) and is again an extension of Heron's machine (4). In an English translation the machine is described as a 'Very subtil engine to raise Water by means of the sun', which according to its inventor 'hath great effect in hot places, as in Spain or Italy; because in those places the sun shines almost always with great heat especially in the summer' (5). The illustration fig. 1.9 is basically the same as fig. 1.4 but the necessary non-return valves are clearly shown. The apparatus was to consist of:

> four copper vessels (the engraving only shows two of them, n,n) well soldered round about, each of which must be about a foot square, and eight or nine inches high. A pipe S,S is placed in each vessel, having other pipes W.W attached to it, reaching almost to its bottom, a sucker valve, Z is placed in the middle of the pipes, made and placed so that, when the water springs out of the vessels, it may

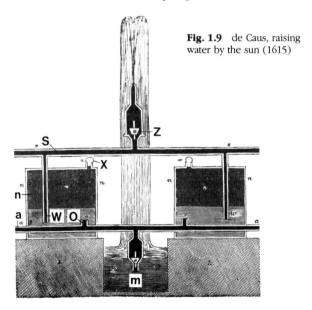

Fig. 1.9 de Caus, raising water by the sun (1615)

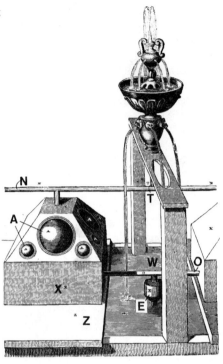

Fig. 1.10 de Caus, raising water by the sun (1615)

open, and being gone forth, may shut again. You must also have another pipe a,a with small pipes, o,o rising upwards at the bottom of these vessels, and also a sucker (or valve) to the end of which there is a pipe m, which descends into the water of the cistern r. To the copper vessels n,n, there shall also be vent holes x,x. Placing the engine in a place where the sun may shine upon it, pour water into the vessels n,n, by the holes x, to about a third part of their content; the air with which they were previously filled will pass out by the passages. Afterwards you must stop all these passages; and the sun shining upon the engine shall make an expression because of the heat, which causeth the water to rise from all the vessels by pipes w,w and pass forth by the valve z; and when there shall be a great quantity of water run forth by the violence of the heat of the sun, then the valve z shall return; and after the heat of the day is passed, and the night shall come, the vessels, to shun vacuity, shall draw up the water of the cistern by the pipes a,o,m and shall fill the vessels as they were before, so long as there may be any water in the cistern.

However, this system could not have been too successful as the translator goes on to state that if the water is to be raised five or six feet then 'the foregoing engine cannot raise it if the sun does not shine with great violence . . . to increase the force of the sun' he proposes to improve the 'Subtil Engine' by fitting burning glasses A,A into the sides of the copper vessels (fig. 1.10). The glasses were to be placed towards the south and west so 'that the sun shining upon them may assemble the rays of the sun within the said vessels, which will cause a great heat to the water and by that means make it spring forth with great abundance'.

X is the copper vessel communicating by the pipe O, with pipe and valve E in the cistern W. N,N are pipes in which the water rises through T, into the fountain placed over it. Z is a floor over the cistern for supporting the copper vessels.

The idea for using lenses to increase the force of the sun may have come from the practice of distilling water by the action of the sun's rays with or without lenses. Porta describes this method in his tenth book of *Natural Magic*, observing that 'the waters extracted by the sun are best'.

The action of the weather glass was commented on by Robert D'Acres who in 1669 published his treatise on:

THE
ELEMENTS
OF
WATER-DRAWING
OR A

Compendious abstract of all sorts and kinds of Water-Machines or Gins, used or practised in the World, with their natural grounds and reasons, and what service may be expected from them.

As also new and exquisite ways and Machins never before published.

With a Philosophical discourse, and new discovery of drawing water out of great deeps by fier.

Where is also disapproved.

The perpetual motion,
The water-poise,
The Syphon or Philosophers Engine,
The horizontal sails,

With divers other experiments.

Published for the improving the service of the Mineral
World, for supplying our most necessary wants of firing,
for raising of water for Cities and Town,
and for watering and draining of grounds.

– in which he puts forward a proposal for raising water by means of
fire (8). Before so doing he considered the power of the sun in raising
water to the clouds and in practicable terms considered that 'Doubt-
lesse most Distillatory glasses are perfect patterns of those celestial
performings, such also are those weather glasses, only some what
extream upon the lesser hand, best, and usefullest mean for this design
(I conceive) is between them both'.

D'Acres was aware of the (then) recent experiments with the mercury
barometer. Knowing that his machine would not raise water above
thirty two feet he stated that he 'expected no more from it and would be
content with less'.

The following is his proposition (fig. 1.11):

> For the conveniency, or expeditious actings hereof, the best and
> most appropriate Heatings and Coolings are to be chosen, and the
> most speedy applications thereof. The best heating, is by the
> incensed Air of a close furnace; The speediest Cooling by water,
> Which though it be not in its self an Element so cool as Earth usually
> is, nor as Air some times is, yet it hath a maintaining Coolnesse,
> which seconds these former acts according to the quantity of the
> adjoyning water, which may easily be exceeding much: For the
> speedier Intercourse of these two contraries, the one may be
> applyed within side; the other without side the cilinder, or Region of
> the Air: The cooling water may not enter, for then it necessarily
> frustrates the ascent of the water; the heated Air out of the furnace
> may enter (by the turning of a Cock) into the Boul, and so the heat is
> acted in an instant; Then the materials and Globe being all overhead
> in a Pond or Cistern of water, they (after the heat by the returning of
> the Cock is diverted) do as speedily cool, and so the rarified Air
> condensing, the water ascends, and having a brazen Sucker or Clack
> in the bottom, it can not go out again, but by the turning the Cock,
> the uppermost water issues forth, by the sucker in the spout, which
> now the descending water thrusts open, and in the same Act the
> enflamed Air follows after; return the Cock, and the water ascends as
> before. Thus the work is expeditious, and two of these will maintain
> a constant delivery of water, according to the largenesse or number
> of Canes or Pipes fixed to the Tun of Lead or Copper vessel, wherein
> the Air is contained.

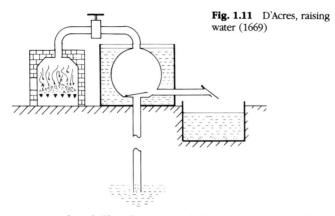

Fig. 1.11 D'Acres, raising water (1669)

Apprehend (for the present) that the water in those aforesaid Actings is not every time all exhausted from the bottom, but that it standeth (from below) fully up, unto the Spout or delivering place, in manner of a sucking Pump, by reason of one or more suckers placed in the Cane or Pipe; and the condensing Air exhausts it from that level, some two or three foot higher, into a bigger bore, or wider barrel (wherein it necessarily lifteth the whole weight from the bottom, as other sucking works do:) And the water thus raised into to the wider place, above the spout (whose sucker is now drawn close) by the turning of the fire Cock, falls violently upon the said sucker, thrust it open, and issuing forth, draws the inflamed Air after it; so that in this Act the venting of the water, and the heating of the Region, or boul, are both at one time. Neither is there any lesse time betweene the cooling and heating: for when you cease to heat, the cooling begins his drawing, and continues raising the water more and more till you give it leave to descend forth, by letting in the warm Air; so that in all these things; as there is not much scruple, nor mater of doubt in the thing it self to be made, so there is lesse question to be made of the manner of accomplishment in a serviceable way: Only (as I am apt to perswade my self) the design pincheth chiefly, if not solely, upon utility: which indeed ought to be the primum mobile, an the chief end of all such designes, (for publick good cannot generally be maintained without privat profit) and without which they are like the tricks of Tumblers, (matters of strangenesse without worthinesse,) And it may be that this politick respect, hath occasioned the suppressing of the work in long inhabited Lands where firing beares a great rate, than will be (with profit) afforded: And thence (happily) this business proves like the Counsell of Cafius the Physician in

Tiberus the Emperours time, which was to remedy a general Head-ach, caused by sitting so near Coal fires (as they conceived;) advising them to quench the Coals with wine, and then they would prove lesse hurtful and offensive; had our times and countries the wine, they would warm themselves first therewith without the fire, though their heads should Ake much. Even from our businesse, the remedy may be suspected to be worse than the cure, and we had rather have the fire without the coal. However men generally (especially being not of a divine Philosophical spirit) are soon terrified from good (especially first attempts) and may not without just cause suspect the profit of this work in some phansied strange way of Acting the same. Yet if this aforesaid may be rightly apprehended you cannot conceive the charge to be anything near unto what is commonly defrayed in the motion caused by men or horses: certainly therefore the fuel, nor attendance of this fire cannot be very expensive.

There is also another excellency (which much mitigates both the charge, and anxious vexations that attend works of this nature) in that the instruments of the work are not in any violent motion, and thence break not, nor so much decay; for most of the instruments are fixed, and move not. The Fire and Water (mainly) are the busie bodies. The standing Charge of Erecting this work, will not much exceed the charge of those we use: and it will always be accommo-dated to crooked, narrow, small pits and places, where most of those the world useth cannot. And lastly, when the work is ended, it will return from the brasse or lead therein imployed, some near proportion of what was expended.

Thus I have shewed you what this Element of Fire hath done in great, will do in small, and most probably may do in mean proportions.

D'Acres was not alone at this time in his investigations in drawing water by means of fire. In 1631 David Ramsey had taken out a patent (no. 50) 'To raise Water from Lower Pitts by Fire', and Edward Somerset was also at work on his water-commanding engine for which he received an act of Parliament in 1663.

Heron's temple door engine appeared in a modified form in a proposal put forward by the French physicist Guillaune Amontons (1663-1705). In 1699 Amontons submitted to the French Academy of Science a design for a fire mill (9). His engine was to consist of two drums, one outer, one inner, the outer a cylindrical copper drum 31ft 10in in diameter and 12ft in width, to be subdivided up into 12 compartments. The inner drum was to be of wood and 12ft in diameter by 2ft wide. Each of the twelve compartments was fitted with a flap valve that opened only downwards. The outer drum was to communicate with the inner by means of copper tubes as shown in fig. 1.12. The inner drum was partly filled with approximately 754 cu ft of water weighing some 13,302 (French) pounds. The apparatus could be alternately heated and cooled by a fire and water bath. As a compartment of the outer drum is exposed to the fire the enclosed air is heated and expands, so acting on the water contained in the inner drum, driving the water out through the flap valve into the next compartment, which has the effect of overbalancing the wheel, causing it to revolve. A fresh outer compartment is now exposed to the fire; the water is driven round the inner drum, being unable to return because of the flap valves. Amontons estimated that the wheel would revolve once every 39 seconds and give out 39hp (he estimated that the power of a horse was equal to about 14,000ft lb per minute, and this he considered equal to the effort of six men). His design and estimates on the expected power output were quite theoretical but he seems to have been entirely convinced of the practicability of a 'fire engine'; the cannon, he pointed out, was such an engine and if the power of fire can be used to give such violent action, can it not also be used to drive machinery? This analytical approach to the problem of the heat engine

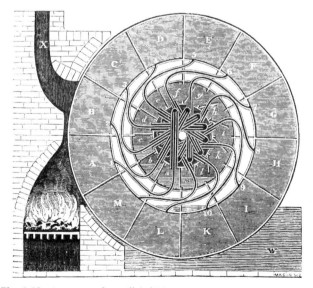

Fig. 1.12 Amontons, fire mill (1699)

was novel, for it showed that Amontons understood the general principles involved, and also that an idealized engine could be used to calculate thermo-mechanical processes, anticipating by 125 years the work of another Frenchman, Sadi Carnot.

In 1702 Amontons had investigated the effects of temperature on the pressure of a gas, but not having an accurate thermometer and in the absence of an established thermometric scale, he made an estimate that air expands or its pressure increases by about one third between the temperature of boiling and cold water. His work, however, was forgotten and only re-disovered after the work of Charles (1787) and Guy Lussac (1802) showed that the volume of a gas, at constant pressure, increases uniformly with its temperature (by $\frac{1}{273}$ of its volume at 0°C, for every degree rise in temperature – Charles Law). Amontons on discovering that air will expand in proportion to its density given the same degree of heat declared '. . . that the spring and weight of the air, with moderate degree of warmth, may enable it to produce even earthquakes and other of the most vehement commotions of nature' (mem. de l'acad 1703).

In 1606 Robert Boyle had published the results of his experiments on the natural spring of air, showing that the product of pressure and volume is always the same. As Boyle always worked at the same temperature that is as far as he got. Similar results were published in 1676 by Mariotte, who had not heard of Boyle's work. The explanation of Boyle was at that time not fully understood: it was common to think of the particles of air as having little springs on them, and when measuring the spring of air it was thought that one was measuring the springs that held them apart. Amontons saw the elasticity of air in terms of the heat or 'fire' it contained. To compress air it was a matter of driving out the 'fire' contained in the gas, and as it would be impossible to remove all of the fire one could go on compressing gas indefinitely. The full explanation did not come until much later when the kinetic theory of gases was developed in the nineteenth century by Maxwell and others.

Another variation on Heron's design appeared in a patent taken out in 1792 (no. 1929) by Thomas Parker for a:

Certain instrument, engine, or machine to be wrought by means of air and water, or by air, fire and water, by which any of the works may be performed as can be done by mills.

In Parker's engine (fig. 1.13) a wheel similar to an inverted water wheel is immersed in a cistern of water, P is a forcing pump or bellows, that passes air through a pipe set over a fire F, and the heated air is then

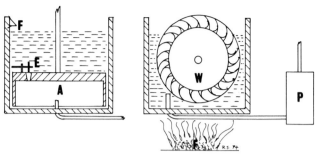

Fig. 1.13 Parker, buoyancy engine (1792)

discharged into the cistern. The heated air displaces water from the buckets, so causing the wheel to revolve, the air pump being in turn driven from the wheel. The mechanical advantage is derived from the fact that the warmed air would displace a greater volume of water than the cold air delivered by the pump. As an alternative to the wheel Parker proposed an air vessel A receiving air in the same way as the buckets of the wheel. The expanding hot air would displace water from beneath the vessel which by its increased buoyancy would be driven upwards. A valve E is fitted to the top of the vessel so that when it strikes the stop F the air would be allowed to escape and the vessel sink to the bottom to be again filled with air. Parker concluded his patent with the notion that the power might be further increased by covering the water cistern but leaving an opening through which the air might escape; a fan then placed in this opening could then be powered by the escaping air and steam.

A very similar design to that of Thomas Parker was patented in 1810 by Mark Brunel (no. 3384). Brunel patented his engine as 'an Invention communicated to him from a certain foreigner living abroad', and that certain foreigner was almost certainly fellow Frenchman Cagnard-Latour, who had a report of his engine presented to the Classe des Science et Physiques et Mathematics of the Institute Nationale on the 8th May 1809 (11, 12). The report was presented by Messrs de Prony, Charles, Montgolfier and Lazare Carnot.

Cagnard's engine consisted of an inverted bucket wheel completely immersed in hot water, the wheel driving an Archimedean screw immersed in a separate reservoir of cold water with just the top open to the air. As the screw turned air was driven to the bottom of the reservoir and by means of an inverted funnel collected and conveyed via a pipe to the bottom of the vessel containing the wheel. As in Parker's engine air displaced water from the buckets in the wheel and by its buoyancy drove the wheel round. The height of the column of cold water

21

(measured from the base of the inverted funnel to the surface of the hot water) was such that it exceeded the height of the hot water in order that the pressure of water drove the air from one vessel to the other. Cagnard found that the power to drive the screw was three pounds at a velocity of 1in per second and this gave rise to an output from the wheel of 15lb at the same velocity. Thus the effect of air taking up heat was to give rise to a surplus of power equal to 12lb at a velocity of 1in per minute, i.e. 36lb per minute or four times what would be required from an external source to keep the machine in motion. The water was heated to 167°F, so presenting an ideal opportunity of utilising sources of waste heat, and because the wheel and pump were immersed in water they were effectively reduced in weight, so reducing the frictional losses in the bearings. Although the engine was slow it ran with a uniformity of motion and was simple in design, so that, to quote Brunel's patent, its working 'cannot but be obvious to any millwright or competent person', and it is one of the first documented cases of an engine working on the principle of compressing cold air isothermally then heating and expanding the air isothermally. As a method of utilizing the expansive powers of heated air this design was too inefficient to have become a practical engine.

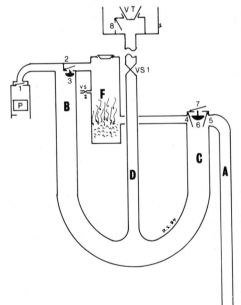

Fig. 1.14 Montgolfier, raising water (1816)

In a design by A. L. Normandy a bucket wheel was to be immersed in molten lead! (UK patent 633, 1867).

Brunel was also involved in another experimental engine. On 14th March 1816 a patent was granted to Pierre Montgolfier for improvements in hydraulic rams (no. 3395) and, with Louise Dayme, a patent (no. 3395) for a 'Machine which acts by the expansion or contraction of air heated by fire, applicable to the raising of water or for giving motion to mills and other machines.' The machine took the form of a hydraulic ram where the driving force was to be heat instead of gravity. In 1815 Montgolfier had come to England and enlisted the help of Mark Brunel, who undertook extensive experiments for him. Although Montgolfier was convinced as to the feasibility of the scheme, the experiments in the end proved a failure, since for a given quantity of heat, the engine showed no advantage over the steam engine. A contemporary description of the engine gives the vessels, in which the fires burnt, as standing some considerable height and some 8 to 10ft in diameter so that large volumes of heated air could be employed, and a considerable quantity of water was raised some 20 to 30ft in height.

The engine consisted of an enclosed furnace through which air was passed, heated and so increased in pressure. This increase in conjunction with a subsequent contraction of the air was used to set up oscillations in a vertical column of water which in its ascent drew up a quantity of water and took in a fresh charge of air, and threw up the water into a reservoir. On its return or descent the water column expelled the spent gases from the furnace by driving in a fresh charge of air. For the engine to work the expansion of air in the furnace needed to be very rapid to give momentum to the column of water and intake of fresh air had to be done very quickly. Montgolfier and Dayme seem to have been abreast of current developments in air engines since they ascribed the development of a closed furnace for heating air to Sir George Cayley, who had built an air engine some ten years previously, and had published his design in 1807.

A simplified layout is shown in fig. 1.14, not to scale. Valves no. 1, 2, 4, 5 and 7 are simple non-return valves. Valves no. 3 and 6 are float valves closed by the water level rising in chambers C and B. F is a closed furnace fitted with valve VS2. A is the riser from the sump and D the delivery pipe fitted with valve VS1. P is a loose fitting piston in a cylinder and is used to meter the fresh charge of air into the engine. Suppose a vacuum be applied to valve 1, it will open and P be sucked up until it closed the orifice of V, allowing no more air to be drawn in through V1. A quantity of air equal to the volume of the cylinder above P will have been drawn in; to vary the quantity of air, the position of P need only be moved up or down in its cylinder. The valves V1, 2, 3 and furnace F are placed in a position higher than valves V4, 5, 6 and 7.

The mode of operation was as follows:

1. With chambers A, B, C, D full of water and valves VS1 and VS2 open,

2. To start the engine depress V6, which will allow water to escape through V6 and V7 so lowering the level in chamber B. Air will then be sucked in through V1, drawing up P till it blocks V1 and no more air will be drawn in and so V6 can be released. P will then slowly fall back.

3. Chamber B is now full of air and chamber C full of water.

4. Valve VS2 is now closed and VS1 open, the weight of the vertical column of water in D will now compress the air in B and force it through valve V2 into the furnace where it will rapidly become heated.

5. The air pressure will now rise, V4 will open and the air will drive the water out from chamber C. (V6 is already closed by the water level in C and will be kept closed by the air pressure.) Water will be forced rapidly up outlet pipe D. The water level in B will rise until float valve V3 is closed and expansion ceases.

6. Chamber B is now full of water and C full of heated air.

7. The water in D will by its momentum continue to rise. The air pressure in C will now begin to fall. Valve V6 will open and V7 will simultaneously close. A fresh charge of air is then drawn in through valve V1.

8. Chamber C is now full of warm air and B full of cold air. Valve V3 will open and V2 close.

9. The momentum of the water in D will further reduce the pressure in B and C causing valve V5 to open, drawing up water in pipe A. The ingress of cold water through V5 into chamber C will further cool the air in C, drawing up more water.

10. When the water finally loses energy for upward movement it will start to fall, causing the spent gases to be driven out through V7 until the rising water closes float valve V6.

11. Chamber C is now full of water and B full of air. The air in B will be compressed and forced into the furnace and the cycle repeated.

12. To enable a sudden expansion of air to take place and so impart rapid movement of the water in D a toggle valve VT was fitted to the top of the outlet pipe. The pressure in the furnace would rise until it overcame the valve which would then pop open and the water be rapidly driven up the pipe D, a non-return valve V8 being fitted to allow the water to fall back down again. As in a conventional hydraulic ram the size of the delivery pipe D would have to be made long enough to ensure that sufficient mass of water was put into motion to act as a fluid

flywheel. Montgolfier's engine worked on an open cycle and, as John Ericsson was to find some forty years later with his 'caloric engine', is less efficient and with the need for valves more troublesome than an engine built on a closed cycle. A closed cycle engine has been developed by Harwell Research Laboratory and is very simple when compared with the Montgolfier engine (UK patent 1329567). A diagrammatic layout is shown in fig. 1.15. D is the drive pipe, H and C a connecting pipe, one end hot, the other cold, A and B the two legs of a bent tube.

1. At rest A and B are half full of water.

2. If H is now heated, the internal air pressure will rise and water will be driven out through D. This will have the effect of lowering the water level in A.

3. Since the level in B is higher than that in A water will flow from B into A, the air in A will flow from A into B and on passing through C be cooled.

4. The internal air pressure will now fall and water will be sucked back along D into A. The level in A will now rise further causing the enclosed air to be compressed into B, the cold chamber of the engine.

5. Level A is now higher than that of B and water will flow from A into B and the enclosed air be driven from B to A passing through H to become heated.

6. The internal air pressure will now rise and water be driven out along D. Rapid motion is imparted to the water in D, which will act as a fluid flywheel so that water will continue to flow out of the engine after

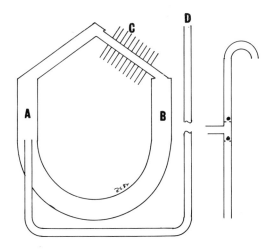

Fig. 1.15 Harwell, water pump (1970)

the internal pressure equals that outside, so further lowering the water level in A.

7. Movement in D will then cease, water in B is now higher than in A so water will flow into A and the internal pressure begins to fall. Water will now be sucked back along D. Due to the momentum of the water in D water will continue to flow after the pressure inside the engine equals that outside. The level in A will rise above that in B and so compress the air into B.

8. Level in A will now fall and that in B rise, so continuing the cycle.

As in any air engine the dead space in the engine must be kept to a minimum. A small model built by the author was not found to be self-starting and the length of drive pipe D was fairly critical. After an hour or so the engine stopped due to the internal air being absorbed into the water.

A full description of modern liquid piston engines can be found in reference 18.

The idea of using the expansive powers of hot gases directly on to the surface of water was used in waterworks in the last century but an explosive mixture of town gas and air was used (see UK patent 653. 9/3/1863 – P. Hugan, 'Pumping water by hot gases'). A popular design is the Humphrey pump developed by H. A. Humphrey in 1906 (UK patent 20,736).

Possibly the first commercial application of pumping water by the direct action of hot gases was by Samuel Brown. Brown was granted two patents (UK patent 4874, 1823 and patent 5350, 1826) for 'An engine or instrument for effecting a vacuum and thus producing power by which water may be raised and machinery put into action'. The engines took the form of gas vacuum machines.

In 1824 a model engine built by Brown was reported as capable of lifting 300 gallons of water for 1 cu in of gas.

In a circular dated 1st May 1832 Brown referred to engines in constant and successful operation.

1. On the Croydon Canal for raising water from a lower to higher level.

2. At Soham, in Cambridgeshire, for the drainage of the Middle Fen District.

3. At Brown's works at Eagle Lodge, Old Brompton, Middlesex. The Croydon engine is shown in fig. 1.16.

A is a wrought iron cylinder, 22ft high and 3ft 6in in diameter, standing in the lower level T of the canal. To set it to work, water is turned on by the cock B on the wheel C (which regulates the

26

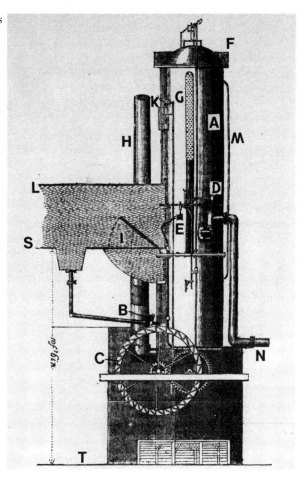

Fig. 1.16 Brown's gas engine (1832)

motions and the number of strokes per minute) which opens the valve D and admits a certain quantity of gas into the cylinder: this is immediately inflamed by a jet of lighted gas, E, and expels the air from the cylinder by raising the lid F, which then instantly shuts; and the perforated tube G, which is fed by the outer pipe H, giving out its water, cools the cylinder instantly, completes the vacuum and raises the water in the cylinder 7ft above the discharge nozzle I, and the upper level S; the atmospheric valve K is then opened, and the water rushes out of the discharge valve I into the canal through the shoot L, and the stroke completed. The height to which the water ascends in

27

the cylinder is indicated by the glass tube M, N is the pipe from the gasometer.

The gas for the engine was made on site, and the sale of by-products in the form of coke and tar provided a profit to the canal company, as the following (drawn up in 1832) shows:

CROYDON GAS ENGINE ACCOUNT

Dr	£. s. d.	Cr	£. s. d.
To 50 bushels small coal at 22s per chaldron for 24 hrs or 417 chaldron for 300 days.	458.14.0	By 35 bushels best coke from ovens, or 292 chaldron in 300 days	379.12.0
To 1 man to attend the engine, 5s per day and 3s coal per week	85.16.0	By 36 bushels coke from retorts or 300 chaldron in 300 days, 22s	330. 0.0
To repairs of machinery, ovens, retorts &c, 2s per week	4. 4.0	By 16 gallons tar, in 24 hours, 4,800 gallons in 300 days, at 3d	6. 0.0
To seven per cent on value of building	35. 0.0		
To ground rent of premises	7. 0.0	Deduct Dr account	666.14.0
	£666.14.0	To profit and loss	£102.18.0

The canal company had previously paid £273 per annum to run a steam engine. The Croydon canal opened in 1809 and closed in 1836 when parts of the canal bed were turned over to railway tracks.

Two engines were erected at Eagle Lodge. The first, termed a pillar engine, was similar to the Croydon engine. The cylinder was 4ft 8½in in

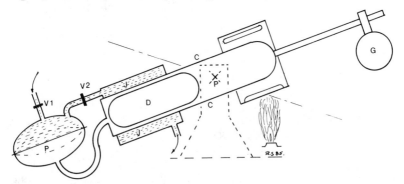

Fig. 1.17 Kuhne, water pump (1887)

28

diameter. It gave four and five strokes per minute, and raised in four strokes as much water from a depth of 12ft, as filled a tank of 3000 gallons capacity, the water rose 6½ft above the discharge nozzle giving a total lift of 18½ft. The second engine was constructed like a beam engine, the gas vacuum apparatus connected to a piston at one end of the beam, with the other end of the beam connected to a pump for lifting water.

A variation on the overbalancing type of engine is found in a patent granted to P. A. Kuhne, from Dresden, Saxony, in 1887 (UK patent 9506) for an improved Hot-Air pumping engine and Motive power engine. The invention (fig. 1.17) consisted of a cylinder C containing a free moving displacer D. The cylinder was supported on trunnions P so that it could rock back and forth. One end of the cylinder was to be cooled by a water jacket J while the other end was heated. To balance the cylinder an adjustable weight was fitted to the hot end. To the cold end a diaphragm pump P was attached fitted with valves V1 and V2, water was drawn in through V1 and forced out through V2 into the cooling jacket. The mode of operation was to be as follows:

1. The balance weight G is adjusted so that when the pump is full of water the cylinder will overbalance to the position shown.

2. The displacer will move to the cold end of the cylinder, shifting the enclosed air to the hot end. The air heat temperature rises and the air pressure acts on the diaphragm of the pump driving out the water.

3. The cylinder now will overbalance and the displacer moves to the hot end, shifting the air to the cold end.

4. The air now cools and air pressure falls and the diaphragm draws water into the pump body.

5. The weight of water now overbalances the cylinder, the displacer moves to the cold end and the cycle repeats.

The inventor claimed that 'In this manner the apparatus operates noiselessly from 30 to 40 times per minute, according to its construc-

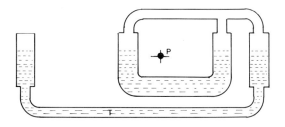

Fig. 1.18   Harwell, liquid piston (1970)

tion'. A similar form is that designed about 1970 by the UKAEA (patent 132957) where a U tube, having one leg hot and the other cold, rocks back and forth, around a pivot P, displacing fluid from one leg to the other (fig. 1.18). A retaining spring keeps the device in equilibrium. In an experimental engine water was used as the displacer fluid in the U tube amd mercury in the balance tube T. The swept volume per leg was approximately 3 cubic centimetres with a temperature difference of 60°C and operating frequency of one half cycle per second.

An interesting form of Heron's solar engine appeared in the *English Mechanic* for 1st February 1901. The following description, a method of storing solar energy in the form of raised weights, was given for driving a long case clock, and the writer, a Clerkenwell watchmaker, related that:

> It is run by no less a power than the Solar system itself, and approaches as nearly to the idea of perpetual motion as anything I know. Briefly Mr Burton availed himself, in the following manner, of the well-known properties of heat and cold to expand and contract air. Upon the average there is a difference of 20 deg in the night and day temperatures. Mr Burton placed a tin tank 10ft high by 9in in diameter upon a sunny wall of his house. From this tank, which is air-tight, a tube runs into a cylindrical reservoir in his cellar. In this reservoir is a piston, the rod of which moves with a ratchet between the chain on which the piston depends. This ratchet winds the clock (an old grandfather pattern) in the following manner. The expanding heat of the day acts upon the outside tank, and forces part of the contained air into the reservoir below. Simultaneously the piston is forced upwards. With the approach of night, however, the air in the outside tank rapidly cools and shrinks; the air in the reservoir once more ascends before the weight of the piston, and the ratchet is again put into motion. This ratchet controls the old-fashioned weights by means of which the clock is wound and the clock will consequently wind and rewind so long as the heat and cold endure and its bearings refrain from wearing out.

There have been many designs for perpetual clocks, some using an earth battery or, as in the clocks built by James Cox, changes in barometric pressure, to provide the power.

The previous design worked a rate of one cycle per day, but in a design by R. A. Fessenden of Brant Rock, Massachusetts, USA, again for storing energy, by raising water to a height to be later discharged through a turbine, water was to be continually raised by solar heat (UK patent 14,745, 1907). The solar pump was to be formed of a sealed

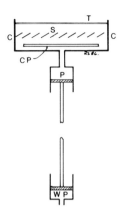

Fig. 1.19 Fessenden, solar
pump (1907)

chamber C fitted with a transparent covering T, below which were fitted
pivoting shutter S and a set of cooling pipes CP. Air contained in C acts
on a piston P to which is connected a water pump WP (fig. 1.19).

The mode of operation was as follows:

1. Solar heat warms the air in C which then acts on piston P driving it
and the water pump down.

2. The shutters are then closed and cooling water passed through CP.
The air pressure now drops causing the piston of the engine and pump
to rise.

3. The shutters now open and the cycle is repeated.

2 Ventilating furnaces, smoke jacks and hot air balloons

Man's first use of heat was in open fires for cooking and giving warmth. As man learned to control fire it was noticed that the hot gases from the fire rose up into the air. From the works of Aristotle (c. 280 BC) we know that the Greeks appreciated that warm air has a natural buoyancy and will rise above cooler air (1). In practical terms this knowledge was first used in improving the design of fireplaces and chimneys. In a book on Architecture, written about 45 BC, by a Roman engineer named Vitruvius the following recommendations for the building of hot baths are given (2).

> The hanging floors of hot baths are to be made as follows: first the ground floor is to be paved with eighteen inch tiles sloping towards the furnace so that when a ball is thrown in it does not rest within but comes back to the furnace room itself. Thus the flames will more easily spread under the floor.

When a fire is placed in a grate set beneath a well-designed chimney it will burn much more strongly, since the hot gases from the fire as they rise up the chimney cool and so suck in fresh air to the grate. In fact quite large volumes of air can be moved, depending on the height of the chimney and strength of the fire. The most obvious use is in the heating and ventilating of buildings and an early domestic use was in Roman dwellings and bath houses. In larger buildings clay pipes carried warm air from a central furnace under the floor and up through the walls. Such comforts were the prerogative of the rich and with the fall of the Roman Empire the system fell into disuse and not until recent times has warm air heating come back into use in domestic dwellings, though now a fan is used to move the warm air from a central heater instead of natural convection.

During the early seventeenth century the depth to which coal mines were being driven gave rise to acute problems with ventilation. One solution which was found was the ventilating furnace. Where there existed fire damp this method was not without its dangers, and in those British pits where in low gas mines ventilating furnaces had remained in use up to the early 1950s, the Mines and Quarries Act of 1954 prohibited them from use in pits sunk after this date. With the introduction of two shaft working it had been noticed that there was an alternating flow of air through the workings, changing with the seasons of the year, warm air rising up one shaft and cool falling down the other (3). This led to the hanging of an iron basket of burning coals in one shaft: the first introduction in Great Britain was at Cheadley in North Staffs at about 1650. The original idea may have come initially from Belgium, as in 1665 the 'Belgium' method was described to the Royal Society. The furnace described consisted of a chimney 5ft square and some 28 to 30ft high, placed near the mouth of the shaft to be ventilated, and near the bottom of the chimney was hung an iron cradle full of burning coals, to produce the necessary rising current of warm air. From one side of the chimney, in a single shaft mine, a 9in square air duct was carried down into the mine. At Wallsend pit, in 1789, a furnace was placed at the bottom of the upcast shaft, for here it would give better results since the shaft acted as a very tall chimney. Mines that employed ventilating furnaces could be identified by a short wide stack at the top of the upcast shaft. In some mines the furnace doubled for both ventilating and driving an underground steam engine. In very gassy pits the furnace was a great source of danger because of the high level of fire damp passing over the furnace. Whenever a big fall in the barometer occurred it was necessary to extinguish the fires which were then, because of the danger, only relit under favourable conditions. Usually the fire was charged with coals and highly inflammable material, the miners withdrew from the mine and a red hot iron ring was run down the shaft on a line, or in special cases a slow match was left to fire a train of gunpowder which in turn lit the furnace fire.

Results with ventilating furnaces were variable. In 1835 the furnace in use at Wallsend colliery on the Tyne circulated 5000 cu ft of air per minute while two pits on the Wear could make 49,000 and 96,000 cu ft per minute and by 1850 the Hetton colliery furnace moved 190,000 cu ft of air per minute, the air in the upcast shaft reaching 145°F and the efficiency being 13,600 cu ft of air circulated per pound of coal. To reduce the risk of explosion in some mines the return air entered the upcast shaft by means of a dumb drift set above the furnace which was fed by air of low gas content. The risk of explosion gradually led to furnaces being replaced by steam driven ventilating fans, except in very low gas pits.

The use of fires for ventilating purposes has been the subject of many patents. The first was taken out by Samual Sutton, a brewer from London, for a contrivance for clearing ships' holds of foul air. Sutton proposed to utilise the fire used for the copper or boiling place found in most ships of the time. Under every copper or boiler were two holes separated by a grate, one for the fire and the other for the ashes, and there was also a flue communicating with the fireplace for the discharge of smoke. In order to clear the ship's hold of foul air it was proposed to close off the hole to the fire and ash place with iron doors and to lay copper or lead pipes of sufficient size from the hold into the fireplace and so supply a draught for feeding the fire (4). A constant discharge from the hold was hoped for, with fresh air being drawn down through the hatches. It seems that Sutton had difficulty in getting his idea into use and only after considerable delay managed to obtain a patent. After petitioning King George II he was granted patent no. 602 in 1744 for a:

New invention or method for extracting foul air out of ships, and will equally contribute to the removing of all noxious air what so ever and may be conveniently applied to mines and caverns in the earth, dungeons, prisons and all infected places.

In desert areas solar energy has been used to provide both ventilation and heating by causing convection of air through the rooms in a building. In central Iran buildings are constructed with an air tower, flat roofs and thick walls giving a high thermal storage capacity. In the hot dry summer months cooling is achieved by opening at night windows and dampers (that shut the rooms from the air tower) when the air tower acting as a chimney draws in the cold night air through the windows to cool the building. Air entering through the basement is further cooled by picking up moisture that has diffused in through the ground. In this way the interior of the building and also the air tower is cooled so that during the day hot dry air is drawn down the air tower to be cooled before entering the rooms.

Ventilating stoves for use in buildings came into use in the nineteenth century, being constructed with a view to promoting the circulation and renewal of air as well as heating in apartments (5). One type that was sold in Britain was known as Walker's self-feeding stove.

With an increasing use of gas for lighting many proposals were put forward for removing the products of combustion from buildings. An early design was one put forward by Michael Faraday who stated that his attention was first drawn to the subject by the air at the Athenaeum Club. His design used metal tubes in the form of inverted siphons to conduct the fumes from the gas lamp to a chimney, one leg of the siphon being the glass of the lamp, the other the chimney, the warm air rising up the chimney producing the necessary draught. The design was patented by Robert Faraday in 1843 (UK patent 9697) for 'Ventilating gas burners, and burners for consuming oil and tallow, and other matters'. A very similar design was patented by Dr William Chown (UK patent 12,391) in 1848 for ventilating rooms.

Gas lamps were used for ventilating rooms as early as 1811 and gas appliance manufacturers such as Sugg, Hunt and others made ventilating lamps for use in theatres, banks and other public buildings. The House of Commons was ventilated by gas in 1852 using 64 argand burners to a design patented by Isaac Reddell (UK patent 4035) for 'Lighting the interior of offices, theatres, buildings, houses or any place where light may be required' (6). Another method was to use two flues back to back, one to conduct the smoke from the fire, the other for ventilating (7). The heat from the smoke warmed both flues and the air in the ventilating flue so warmed rose and caused a draught that sucked air from the room connected to the flue. The system was patented by William Walker in 1844 (UK patent 10,183) 'Warming and ventilating apartments and buildings'. As recently as 1983 a patent has been granted for a ventilator of this type. A cylindrical ventilator is designed to fit on the top of a flue or ventilating pipe, the bottom terminating in the room to be ventilated. An electrical coil is built into the device heating the inner metal surface of the cylinder and this in turn warms the adjacent air which rises, drawing the colder and denser air in the flue upward through the ventilator (8). It is claimed that although the running cost would be higher the capital cost would be far lower.

The first use of rising air to give mechanical movement seems to have been in China. Rising currents of warm air were evidently used by Ting Huan (c. 180 AD) who made a nine storey hill-censer, on which many strange birds and animals were attached, the creatures moving when the lamp was lit. A similar apparatus, in which moving shapes and tinkling noises are heard after lighting the lamp, is mentioned in the tenth century AD. Sung scholars Fan Cheng and Chiang Khuei both wrote poems describing how with the ma chhi teng (horse riding lamp) one can see the shadow horses prancing around, after the lamp is lit. A similar prancing horse lamp is referred to in a description of

Hangchow written in 1275. Gabrial Magalhaens wrote of them in the middle of the seventeenth century:

> . . . the lamps and candles, of which there are an infinite number in every Lanthorn, are intermixed and placed with-in-side, so artificially and agreeable, that the light adds beauty to the painting; and the smoke gives life and spirit to the figures in the Lanthorn, which Art has so contrived, that they seem to walk, turn about, ascend and descend. You shall see horses run, draw chariots and till the Earth; Vessels sailing; Kings and Princes go out with large trains; and a great numbers of people both a-foot and a-horse back, Armies marching, Comedies, Dances, and a thousand other Divertisements and Motions represented . . .

Modern writers have described toys of this kind being made in China, especially in Peking. Tun Li-chhen writing in 1900 on annual customs and festivals of Peking said:

> Prancing-horse lamps are wheels cut out of paper, so that when they are blown on by (the warm air rising from) a candle (fastened below the wheel), the carts and horses (painted on it) move and run round and around without stopping. When the candle goes out the whole thing stops. Though this is but a trifling thing, it contains in truth the whole underlying principle of completion and destruction, rise and decay, so that in the thousand ages from antiquity down to today, as recorded in the Twenty-four Histories, there is not one which is not like a prancing-horse lamp.

The principle is still used today in modern table lamps where the heat from an electric light bulb rises to turn the lamp shade. They are to be found in public houses advertising beer, in children's bedrooms showing animated scenes from children's stories, or at Christmastime the heat from burning candles sends brass angels spinning round to strike small bells.

Smoke jacks

In the fifteenth century there appeared in the kitchens of Europe a new machine to drive the roasting spits common at this time. The origin of the smoke jack is uncertain, but the idea may have come from the East (10). An example is found in the works of Leonardo da Vinci (1452-1519), dated possibly about 1480 (11). A fan is placed in the chimney

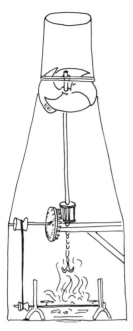

Fig. 2.1 da Vinci,
Smoke jack (c1480)

Plate 3 A preserved smoke jack

above the kitchen fire so that the rising hot gases caused it to turn
(fig. 2.1). The fan is geared to the spit via lantern gearing and belt drive.
Leonardo insisted that this was the right way to cook meat since the
spit would revolve faster or slower according to the fierceness of the
fire. The fan he used bears a little resemblance to contemporary
drawings of windmills or helicopter toys.

The smoke jack appears in the works of Carden published in 1548
(12). Jerome Carden was a Milanese and well acquainted with the works
of da Vinci (fig. 2.2). John Wilkins quotes from Carden (13). After
referring to the action of windmills and eolipiles the learned bishop has
this to say on smoke jacks:

> . . . but there is a better invention to this purpose mentioned in
> Carden, whereby a spit may be turned (without the help of weights)
> by the motion of the air that ascends the chimney; and it may be
> useful for roasting of many or great joints; for as the fire must be
> increased to according to the quantity of meat, so the forces of the
> instrument will augment proportionally to the fire. In such contri-

37

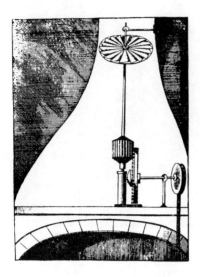

Fig. 2.2 Carden, smoke jack (1548)

vance there are these convenience above the jacks of ordinary use:

1. It makes little or no noise in the motion.

2. It needs no winding up, but will constantly move of itself, while there is any fire to rarifie the air.

3. It is much cheaper than the other instruments that are commonly used for this purpose. There being required with it only a pair of sails, which must be placed in that part of the chimney where it begins to be straightened, and one wheel, to the axis of which the spit line must be fastened to the following diagram (fig. 2.2). The motions of these sails may like wise be serviceable for sundry other purposes, besides the turning of a spit, for the chiming of bells or other musical devises; and there cannot be any more pleasant contrivance for continual and cheap music. It may be useful also for reeling yarn, for rocking of a cradle with the like domestick occasions. For (as said before) any constant motion being given, it is for an ingenious artificer to apply it to various services. The sails will always move both night and day, if there is but any fire under them, and sometimes if there be none, for if the air without be much colder than within the rooms, then must this be warm and rarefied, naturally ascend through the chimney, to give place unto more condensed and heavy, which does usually blow in at every chink or cranny, as experience shows.

By 1572 the smoke jack seems to have become sufficiently well used for

Fig. 2.3 Branca, rolling mill (1629)

it to have been mentioned in a book on cooking written by Barttolmea Scappi, who was cook to Pope Pius 5th, in 1570 (14).

A visitor to Switzerland in 1580 wrote:

> Since the Swiss are excellent workers in iron, almost all of their spits are turned by springs or by means of weights like clocks, or by cert ain broad light sails of pine they place in the funnel of their chimneys, which turn with great speed in the draught caused by the smoke and the steam of the fire: and they roast slowly – for they dry out the meat a little too much. These windmills are used only in the large inns where there is a big fire, as at Baden (on the road from Basel to Zuric) . . . They use almost the whole width of the kitchen for the flue. This is a great opening, seven or eight paces square which narrows as it goes up to the top of the house. This gives them room to place it in one spot their big sail, which with us would take up too much room.'

Vittoria Zonca illustrated a smoke jack in his works (16). He seems to have thought that it was the smoke which did the work, as did Elizabethan mathematician John Dee who spoke of 'Mills by smoke moved'. Giovanne Branca (1571-1640) proposed a small rolling mill to be powered by the heat of the forge; the flyer was to be set horizontally (fig. 2.3) (17).

Samuel Pepys noted in his diary for 1660 that when visiting the house of a Mr Spong: 'After supper he looked over many books and instruments of his, especially his wooden jack in his chimney, which goes with the smoke, which is indeed very pretty'.

By the early nineteenth century the smoke jack was being made along elaborate lines, the fan being connected to a long horizontal shaft above the fireplace, at each end of which were wooden or brass driving wheels for the spits. At intervals along the shaft were suspended the 'dangle-spits'; these by means of the bevel gears revolved in front of the fire. Compared with the spits driven by weights or 'spit-hounds' smoke jacks exhibited an extravagant use of energy. In Loudon's *Encyclopaedia of Architecture*, published in 1833, Count Runford gives his opinions on the smoke jack:

> To complete the machinery of the ordinary British kitchen range, which seems to be calculated for the express purpose of devouring fuel, a smoke jack is generally placed in the chimney,

No human invention, he adds, ever came to his knowledge that was so absurd as this; it would not be difficult to prove, he says:

> . . . that so much less than one thousandth part of the fuel that is necessary to burn in an open fire place, in order to cause a smoke jack to turn a loaded spit, would be sufficient to make the spit go round were the force evolved from the combustion of the fuel, if it were properly directed through the medium of a steam engine.

He goes on to state that:

> besides this wast of fuel it would not be other wise wanted, by the necessity which they create for the a great current of air up the chimney, to prevent it from smoking. This also increases the current of cold air from the doors and windows to the fire place; and thus while the side of the cook next to the fire is burnt the other is chilled. A jack moved by a weight or spring, if roasting must still be performed by the barbarous practice of turning on a spit before an open fire, is much preferable; and the trouble of winding it up which is a general argument against it, is much less trouble than the burning of coal to feed the immense fire that is required to cause a common jack to move.

Many patents have been taken out for various improvements in smoke jacks. John Prosser, a smith from Back Hill in London, made various improvements in the drive from the fan to the spits. So that the reduction gearing offered less obstruction to the air flow, and also a method of ensuring continuous lubrication of the gearing, a worm drive was to be used to couple up the spindle of the fan (UK patents 2064, 1795 and 2982 2982, 1806).

John Braithwait, an engine maker in St Pancras in London, patented a design with a fan or flyer, as he called it, rotating on a horizontal shaft (UK patent 2065, 1795). The flyer was shielded from below in such a way that the rising current of air acted on one side only, and the blades or floats of the flyer, twelve in number, were to be carried on the end of spokes, radiating out from a central hub, and set at an angle of 50 deg to them. The overall diameter was to be some 2ft 6in with the floats 14in wide by some 6in deep. A similar design was patented in 1825 (UK patent 5087) by John Thin, an architect from Edinburgh, but here the floats were fixed in line, not at an angle. The size was to be about 2ft 6in with floats about 12in wide by 10in in depth, the limiting factor being the size of the chimney, and the whole unit was hinged so that it could be swung clear for sweeping the chimney. The smoke jack lasted into this century, for in 1907 at the Skinners Company Hall in Downgate, London, a smoke jack was installed by Benham & Son, which is now exhibited in the Science Museum, London.

An alternative to setting the fan above the fire was to utilise the draught sucked in by the fire. In 1728 a patent was granted to John Payn (no. 505) for 'a new engine to be moved by the pressure of air entering a building where large fires are made use of'. Payn proposed to place a large fan on the outside of the building and the air required for the fire would be sucked in through it, being directed onto the outer part for greater turning motion. Useful, he thought, for grinding corn, moving large hammers and raising water. In 1790 Joseph Haterly took out a patent (no. 1775) for an engine constructed on similar principles; in his machine a sealed furnace was used to draw air through a fan or multiple fans joined to a common axis, the power to be regulated by doors placed above and below the fans.

Solar chimneys

An interesting design for a solar engine was proposed by Isidoro Cabanyes of Escorial, Spain, in a patent granted to him in 1907 (UK patent 20,794). The design was basically a smoke jack set in a tall chimney and powered by air directly heated by the sun (fig. 2.4). The heating chamber was formed of two cones of sheet iron O and I, the outer perforated with holes, 4mm in diameter and set 20mm apart, and painted black. The heating chamber was to be subdivided into several compartments each fitted with a sliding door D that communicated with the chimney. During the day the sector that was in the full sun would have its door opened and as it passed into the shade the door would be closed, while to stop the machine all doors would be closed. The chimney was to be of tubular construction formed of sheet iron painted black. Cabanyes thought a chimney height of 20 to 30 metres would be practicable. The motor itself was formed of 'screws or helices' set in the chimney.

A version of Cabanyes' engine has recently (1982) been constructed in Spain for generating electricity (fig. 2.5) (18). Sited at Manzanares, midway between Madrid and Almeria, the plant consists of a 'Solar Chimney', formed by a central chimney surrounded by a circular greenhouse glazed with transparent material G. Sunlight heats the air within the greenhouse and by convection the air rises up the chimney at some 20 to 60 metres per second. In this 100 kW pilot plant a 200m high chimney stands in the centre of a 250m diameter solar collector that varies in height, from the ground, from 2m at the circumference to 6m at the centre. The chimney diameter is 10.3m and weight 200 tons. The

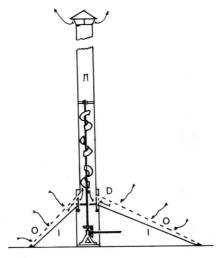

Fig. 2.4 Solar chimney (1907)

construction is made up of 8m long corrugated steel sheets 1mm to 1.25m thick, secured every 4m by annular rings R with a series of 24 guy ropes GR giving support to the structure. Set at the base of the chimney is a variable pitch turbine T having four blades each 5m long. During the day the turbine runs at 1500rpm to produce 100 kW; at night the heat trapped in the ground beneath the collector is given off to power the turbine at a reduced speed of 100rpm, producing 40 kW of electricity. The prototype has been developed under the auspice of the German Ministry for Research and Development, who put aside about £1m of its budget of £8.5m for the Manzanares plant; backing also came from the Spanish utility Union Electric SA.

A breakdown of the costs for this demonstration plant (1979 figures) is given as:

Cost of plastic cover	£380.00
Cost of chimney	£340.00
Turbines and engineering cost	£90.00
Total cost	£810.00
Specific cost (£/kW)	£81.609
Average power with 540W/sq m for a 10 hr day	50 kW
Max. power with 1000W/sq m	100 kW
Average efficiency	0.2%

The ideal locations for solar chimney plants are claimed to be rock deserts where the average solar radiation is between 500 and 600 W/sq m, ample for an almost unlimited supply of power.

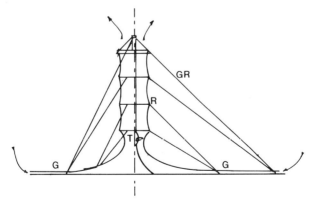

Fig. 2.5 Solar chimney (1982)

Hot air balloons

The power of rarefied air that drove the roasting spits of Europe was to give relief to one of man's greatest desires, that of flight. Several times during the early middle ages writers almost hit upon the hot air balloon. Albertus Magnes (*c* 1200-80) when discussing heaviness and lightness stated that a bladder blown up with warm air from the lungs will be lighter than when empty, but he was only interested in theoretical considerations (19).

Giovana de Fontana writing about 1420 examined the idea for a flying machine that had been put forward by an unidentified predecessor:

> There is one from among those who claim to be inventors and who reason badly, who said that it would be possible for a man to rise into the air by use of some such artifice, and he conceived of making, from thick cloth and rings of wood, a pyramid of very great size whose point would be uppermost, and of firmly tying across the diameter of the circle at the base a bar of wood, on which a man might sit or ride, holding in his hands burning brands made of pitch and tallow or other material producing intense fire which is long-lasting and creates a great deal of thick smoke. He suggests that because of the fire is enclosed within the pyramid it would be made lighter and rarer, and consequently that as it would move upwards and could not, of course, get out, the pyramid and the man sitting in it would be raised; in further support of which he suggested that the vapour from the brands, produced in the pyramid being enclosed and forced up, would rise. He said however that the experiment had not succeeded, either because the pyramid had been too small, or too heavy, or because it had some leak in its cover, because there had been too little of the aforesaid vapour enclosed.
>
> But I was not a little astonished by this man's ideas, and more so than by those of him who proposed descending under the water with the use of a diving-bell. There are indeed many difficulties in this, not to say the greatest danger. In the first place one cannot tell how, in such rare and hot air and in such thick smoke, which should not be lacking from the machine but gather in great quantity, a man might not breath. Again it is to be feared that from so much uncovered fire the pyramid may be burnt up, so causing the burning of the man, or his fall, since the air and the smoke will have been able to escape through the burnt parts of the cloth.
>
> In the third place, if everything he has said up till now be true, one never the less wonders how the man may descend without harm and

danger, since as long as the firebrands are burning the pyramid will rise, but when they have been consumed, with the failer of the motive and sustaining power, the pyramid will be turned back from the air and will rapidly fall downwards, just as things which have been carried up by a whirlwind fall back of their own weight, when the wind drops.

I shall not deal with the remaining difficulties. This man indeed, just like many who presume to begin that which they either do not know how to, nor are able to finish, had not thought his idea out to the end, since as regards the ascent he gave insufficient attention to his reason and arguments, which equally fail to specify the method of descent (20).

Fontana was clearly unimpressed, not having it would seem high opinion of inventors. However, what he relates is clearly a real attempt to fly and is an anticipation of the hot air balloon. It is interesting to note that Leonardo da Vinci made a drawing of a parachute of pyramidal configuration in about 1485, and another drawing by an unknown hand from about 1480 depicts a conical parachute. The failure to lift off the ground was probably due to a lack of awareness of how small is the difference between the density of hot and cold air, and, as with the early parachutes, a failure to understand just how large the machine needed to be.

Possibly the first recorded flight by what may be a hot air balloon was that made by a Jesuit priest, Father Laurenco de Gusmao (1686-1742). There is evidence that he flew a small model, the ascent taking place on 8th August 1709. This information comes from a manuscript (no. 537) in the University Library at Coimbra, and dates from about 1724 (21).

> ... his model consisted of a small bark in the form of a trough which was covered with a cloth of canvas. With various spirits, quintessences and other ingredients he put a light beneath it, and let the bark fly in the Salla das Embaixadas before his majesty and many other persons. It rose to a small height against the wall and then came to earth and caught fire when the materials became jumbled together. In descending and falling backwards it set fire to some hangings and every thing against which it knocked. His majesty was good enough not to take ill.

This scene was also recorded by Father Feereira who described it as 'a globe which rose gently to the height of the Salla . . . raised by a certain inflamable material which the inventor set fire to'. It is not known if Gusmao repeated his experiments.

It was the experiments conducted by two brothers, paper makers in Annonay near Lyons, France, Joseph (1740-1810) and Etienne (1745-99) Montgolfier, that led to the first successful flight by man. Joseph had started experimenting with balloons in 1776, first using hydrogen then hot air. How he came to choose hot air we do not know, but his early experiments were not a success, mainly it seems through lack of a suitable material for the envelope that would keep the gas leakage down to an acceptable level and this led him to seek an alternative. Strangely the Montgolfiers never grasped the real principle behind the hot air balloon, which is when air is heated it expands giving a reduction in density. Instead Joseph believed that combustion produced some kind of gas. Also believing that the quality of gas varied according to the material being burnt, he experimented with various kinds of material, finally settling for a combination of wool clippings and straw to give, he thought, the lightest form of gas.

The first successful model balloon was tested in November 1782 with two more designs being made; the last flew in April 1783, having a diameter of 35ft. These early experiments led the brothers to feel that they had acquired sufficient expertise in the art of balloon building to carry out a public demonstration. With this in mind they set about building a new balloon far larger than any they had so far attempted. It was built in the shape of almost a globe with a circumference of 110ft, and was made of cloth lined with paper reinforced with a network of strings, to the bottom ends of which was attached a square wooden frame surrounding the aperture. It weighed 500lb with a capacity of 22,000 cu ft. The flight took place on the morning of 5th June 1783 in the market place of Annonay, which was crammed with hundreds of people who had come to watch the demonstration. The flight was an unqualified success, lasting 10 minutes, with the balloon travelling about a mile and a half. The flight of so large a balloon was against the then accepted theory that the only known agent light enough to lift a balloon into the air was hydrogen. It became thought that the Montgolfiers had discovered a new and revolutionary type of gas, which came to be called Montgolfier's gas, an assumption strengthened by Montgolfier's belief that the secret lay in the foul smelling combination of wool and straw, as he had still not realised that the air would grow lighter whatever was burnt in the fire (22).

The next demonstration flight was in front of the commissaries of the Academy of Science on the 11th and 12th of September 1783. The new machine was 74ft high and about 43ft in diameter, being made of canvas covered with paper inside and out and weighing some 1000lb. It was heated with a combination of 50lb of dry straw and 12lb of chopped wool, taking about 9 minutes to heat sufficiently. The balloon managed to lift the eight men who held it down some feet off the ground but unfortunately it was damaged by rain. A new balloon had to be built to give a demonstration to the King on the 19th of September. It was constructed of linen and cotton thread and painted both inside and out in water colour, and in size it was near 60ft high and 43ft in diameter. At one o'clock the fire was lit and after some eleven minutes it lifted off. On board were, as passengers, a sheep, a cock and a duck, and they were conveyed some two miles with no harm coming to them.

The success of this first flight led the brothers to consider a manned flight. Work was started on a larger balloon at a site in a garden in the Faubourg St Antoine, the shape being oval instead of the usual spherical, and it was to be 74ft in height by 48ft in diameter. Fitted to the bottom was a wicker gallery some 3ft broad with a balustrade about 3ft high, and hanging from the opening was a grate suspended from chains so that it could be fed with straw from the gallery. On the 15th of October Francois de Rozier climbed on board and tethered test flights were made; on the first the balloon rose 84ft. On the 17th and 19th further flights were made, with the balloon making controlled ascents and descents by controlling the heat of the fire. On the 19th de Rozier was joined by Giraud Villette, taking the balloon to about 330ft. After the successes of the tethered flights the balloon was moved to the grounds of the Chateau la Muette in the Bois de Boulogne. On the 21st November de Rozier, accompanied by the Marquis de Arlands, at 1.54 o'clock lifted off to make man's first free flight in the atmosphere. They were in the air for about 25 minutes and travelled about 1¾ miles across Paris before landing.

In a letter sent to a friend the Marquis described the flight thus:

I was surprised at the silence and the absence of movement which our departure caused among the spectators, and believed them to be astonished and perhaps awed at the strange spectacle; they might well have reassured themselves. I was still gazing, when M. Rozier cried to me: 'You are doing nothing, and the balloon is rising a fathom.' 'Pardon me', I answered, as I placed a bundle of straw upon the fire and slightly stirred it. Then I turned quickly, but already we had passed out of sight of La Muette. Astonished, I cast a glance towards the river. I perceived the confluence of the Oise. And naming the principle bends of the river by the places nearest them, I cried, 'Passy, Saint-Germain, Saint-Denis, Sevres'.

'If you look at the river in that fashion you will be likely to bath in it soon',' cried Rozier. 'Some fire, my dear friend, some fire . . .'

'Look!' I said. At the same time I took my sponge and quietly extinguished the little fire that was burning some holes within my reach. I then perceived that the bottom of the cloth was coming away from the circle which surrounded it. 'We must descend,' I repeated to my companion. He looked below. 'We are on Paris,' he said. 'It does not matter,' I replied. 'Only look! Isn't there any danger? Are you holding on well?'

'Yes I am,' he answered.

I examined the situation from my side, and saw that we had nothing to fear. With my sponge I then tried the ropes which were within my reach. All of them held firm. Only two of the cords had broken. I then said, 'We can cross Paris.' During the operation we were rapidly getting down to the roofs. We made more fire, and rose again with the greatest ease. I looked down, and it seemed to me we were going towards the towers of Saint Sulpice; but, on rising, a new current caused us to quit this direction and bear more to the south. I looked to the left, and beheld a wood, which I believed to be that of Luxembourg. We were traversing the boulevard, and I cried out all at once: 'Get to the ground!' But the intrepid Rozier, who never lost his head and who judged more surely than I, prevented me from attempting to descend. I then threw a bundle of straw on the fire. We rose again, and another current bore us to the left. We were now close to the ground, between two hills. As soon as we came near the earth I raised myself over the gallery, and leaning there with my two hands, I felt the balloon pressing softly against my head. I pushed it back, and leaped down to the ground. Looking round and expecting to see the balloon still distended, I was astonished to find it quite empty and flattened. On looking for Rozier I saw him in his shirt-sleeves creeping out from under the mass of canvas that had fallen over him. Before attempting, to descend, he had taken off his coat and placed it in the basket. After encountering much trouble, we were again all right. As Rozier was without a coat I urged him to go to the nearest house. On his way there, he encountered the Duke of Chartres, who had managed to follow our flight very closely, for I had had the honour of conversing with him just before we ascended.

Sadly de Rozier was to become one of the first two men to be killed in a ballooning accident in 1785; this occurred during an attempt, financed by the French government, to cross the English Channel from France to England, in a combination hydrogen-hot air balloon.

Montgolfier brothers' triumph was to be short-lived, as in December Jacques Charles was to make a flight in a hydrogen-filled balloon, just twenty-six days after the manned flight.

Benjamin Franklin, the American Ambassador to France, who had witnessed both the manned and earlier flights, later commented to Etienne Montgolfier:

> It appears, as you observe, to be a discovery of great importance, and what may possibly give a new turn to human affairs. Convincing sovereigns of the folly of wars may perhaps be one effect of it, since it will be impracticable for the most potent of them to guard his dominions. Five thousand balloons, capable of raising two men each, could not cost more than five ships of the line. And where is the prince who can afford to so cover his country with troops for its defence as that ten thousand men descending from the clouds might not in many places do an infinite deal of mischief before a force could be brought together to repel them?

The Montgolfier brothers went on to build an even larger balloon weighing seven tons, being some 130ft high and 100ft in diameter, giving a capacity of 700,000 cu ft, which carried seven passengers on its maiden flight, including Joseph Montgolfier making his first and only aerial voyage.

Although hydrogen balloons were to take the lead, Montgolfiers continued to be built as they were cheap to construct and in recent years have again come to be built in large numbers with the advent of bottled gas and synthetic cloth. Balloons have also been built using a combination of helium gas and hot air (23).

Perhaps as a shape of things to come, hot air balloons were used by the Austrian army, who laid siege to the city of Venice in 1849, in an attempt to aerially bombard the city. A number of small unmanned balloons were launched, each carrying a 30lb bomb with a slow burning fuse, to float over the city. The plan was that as the air in the balloons cooled the balloons would drop into the city where the bombs would explode. Fortunately for the Venetians the wind changed, but the Austrians took the city anyway.

Hot air balloons make attractive working models and some good designs can be found in *How to Make and Fly Model Hot Air Balloons* (24).

3 Some early designs for piston engines

Wood—Mead—Glazebrook—Carnot

With the advent of Thomas Newcomen's atmospheric steam engine in 1710 the heat engine became a viable proposition and from this time on interest centred on producing power against a piston rather than sucking up water.

James Watt improved on the vacuum steam engine with his separate condenser. While some engineers strove to harness high pressure steam, others produced designs intended to prove greater economies could be made with heated air.

In 1729 a patent (UK patent 507) was granted to Thomas Bewley, a plumber, and Thomas Holtham, a clock maker, both from Coventry for:

> A certain new engine or machine for raising water more extensively by alternate expansion rarefaction, or exhausting of air, and pressure of the atmosphere whereby towns and gardens may be supplied with water and mines, pittes, Docks and fens, etc, may be emptied and drained by more expiditios and cheaper meathod than hath been made invented or used before.

No specification was enrolled so the exact design remains a mystery, though it is of interest to note that a Newcomen engine was erected in 1719 at Wyken near Coventry, followed by a second in 1720 and a third in 1722 (1). The building of these three engines was unlikely to have gone unnoticed by someone in the plumbing trade.

In 1759 a patent was granted to Henry Wood, for 'Working a fire engine upon a principle different to any method hereto fore used and at less than half the expense of coals any method now used requires' (UK patent 739). Henry Wood (1715-95) was vicar of High Ercall, a large parish situated about ten miles from Ironbridge in Coalbrookdale where Abraham Darby had set up his ironworks.

In his patent Wood claims:

I the said Henry Wood, do hereby declare that my invention is to work a fire engine on the principle of hot and rarefied air, produced by the air passing either through fire, or through red hot pipes, or through boiling water, or by any other way heated or rarefied. And whereas hot air may be conveyed into the great cylinder of the engine by different ways, either by the help of bellows or small cylinders, with proper piston and valves, or the pressure of the atmosphere will drive in the air through any heating bodies as the great piston of the engine rises, and so fill the cylinder with hot air, which must be condensed with cold to produce a vacuum, and when condensed must be discharged out of the cylinder; and this discharge may be effected in different ways: if the hot air be driven into the cylinder with a force superior to the pressure of the atmosphere, that force will drive out the condensed air through what is now called the snifting pipe; if the force be only equal, then condensed air must be pump out by a pump; to be worked by the motion of the engine or any other way; therefore, my invention is to work the fire engine by any of the above-recited methods, or by any other way not now in use, whereof hot or rarefied air is the principle, or hot air in conjunction with steam, which must be unavoidable when air is heated by passing through boiling water by the help of pipes.'

In the eighteenth century the area around High Ercall supported numerous coal pits and forges, and it should not be surprising that Wood, with an interest in the Newcomen engine, should enquire as to the fuel consumption. What led him to suppose that he could halve the expense of the engine we do not know, but he must have apprehended that there was something defective in a system that evaporated water only to then condense it to obtain power. A point of interest in the patent is the use of a pump to extract the condensed air; this was to give James Watt problems when actions were brought against Hornblower and others for infringements of Watt's patent, in which Watt claims that 'Whatever air or other elastic vapours is not condensed by the cold of the cylinder and may impede the working of the steam engine, is to be drawn out of the steam vessel or condensers by means of pumps wrought by the engine or otherwise' (UK patent 913, 1769). This would appear to be an infringement of Wood's patent but whether Watt originally knew this is not clear (2).

Thomas Mead, an engineer from Sculcoats in Yorkshire, in a patent granted to him in 1794 (no. 1979) discussed various methods of obtaining motion from repeatedly heated and cooled gases. His idea was to heat air in one chamber where it would expand and act on a piston, then move the gas to a separate chamber where it would be cooled and so contract back to its original volume. The diagram in Mead's patent is shown in fig. 3.1 A is a hollow cylinder, the top being connected via a tube to a valve E which can be adjusted so that A communicates with either funnel C or pipe D. The pipe D fits into F so as to give a sliding airtight fit. The vessel H fits into A so as to give a sliding airtight fit and forms the power cylinder of the apparatus. Valve L can be adjusted to give communication from the atmosphere to the interior of the engine. M is a solid body in the form of two cylinders of unequal diameters joining together in the direction of their diameters and which he calls a transferrer. The lower end is connected to rod N,

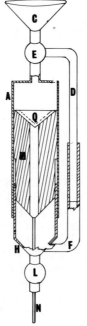

Fig. 3.1 Mead, air engines

and through the displacer is a concentric hole. The lower part of the transferrer is made to fit into H and the upper part into A so as to give sliding fits.

Mead gives several alternatives for operating his engine.

Method 1

Operation by internal combustion and vacuum strokes.

In the top of the transferrer a hollow fire grate Q is placed, of almost equal diameter of the transferrer. Combustible matter is then placed in the grate and ignited. The cycle of events starts with the transferrer M and piston H at the top of their strokes, with valve E closed and L open. The piston then moves down, so drawing in enough atmospheric to support combustion, valve L is now closed. The transferrer is now moved down into H so forcing the enclosed air through the fire causing it to expand and so acting on H drives it down taking M with it. At the bottom of the stroke valve E opens to give communication between A and D. The transferrer M is now returned to the top of its stroke so that the hot gases are moved via pipes D and F back into H where they are cooled, so drawing back up the piston H. When the pressure of enclosed gases and that of the atmosphere become equal valve L opens and H continuing to the top of its stroke drives out the spent gases. Valve E is then closed and the cycle repeated.

Method 2

Operation by internal combustion only.

In this method pipes D and F are dispensed with. The engine starts with H and M at the top of their strokes and valve E shut. H is allowed to descend until enough air has been drawn into the engine then L is closed, the transferrer is then moved down into the piston so causing the enclosed air to be heated, as before, and by expanding drives down the piston and transferrer. At the bottom of the power stroke, valves L and E open, and the piston and transferrer are moved to the top of their strokes so expelling the hot gases. Valve E is then closed and the cycle repeated.

Method 3

Operation with external heating with expansion and vacuum strokes.

In this method pipes D with F and valves L and E also the internal fire grate with fire Q are dispensed with. The top of A is heated externally and H is kept cooled. The transferrer is used to move the enclosed air back and forth from hot to cold ends. When the transferrer moves down the air is shifted into the hot end where it is heated and expands by forcing down the piston, the transferrer is then moved back to its top position so shifting the air into the cold end where it cools and draws back up the piston.

Method 4
Operation with expansion or vacuum strokes.

In this method valves L and E are replaced. With valve E closed and L open and with the transferrer at the top of its stroke the piston is lowered to draw in sufficient air into the engine, L is then closed and the transferrer moved down into H so moving the air into the hot space where it becomes heated and drives down the piston and transferrer. At the bottom of the stroke valve E opens and H and M move upwards so expelling the enclosed heated air. Valve E then closes and L opens and the piston moves down drawing in a fresh charge of air and the cycle is repeated.

To operate on a vacuum cycle, the engine starts with E shut and valve L open and the piston descends to take in a charge of air. Valve L is then closed and the transferrer descends into the piston, the air being then heated and the internal pressure rises as before. Valve E is then opened and the heated air exhausted with some force. (Mead here suggests that the air be directed on the fire to assist in combustion or used where a strong current of heated air is required). Valve E is now closed and the transferrer moved to the top of its stroke so shifting the enclosed air into the cold space where it cools and so draws back the piston.

Mead claimed in his patent that his was not for any particular apparatus, but for methods of obtaining motion from heated and cooled air. It was left to others to realise his ideas for a transferrer piston to shift the air alternately between hot and cold chambers into a practical form.

James Glazebrook, an engineer from Coalbrookdale, sought to increase the elasticity of air so as to give a greater power output (UK patents 2164, 1797 and 2504, 1801). Knowing that different gases have different rates of expansion, Glazebrook realised that the power of his engine was dependent on the type of working gas used. Glazebrook chose to increase the elastic force of compressed air by the application of moisture. In his second patent Glazebrook stated:

As all kinds of airs are not equally expansive, I here insert some of them in their dry or unmoistened state according to their expansive force, beginning with hydrogen, whose expansibility is the least, and which at two hundred and sixty fahrenheit, being divided into one hundred equal parts the others will appear, according to experiment

54

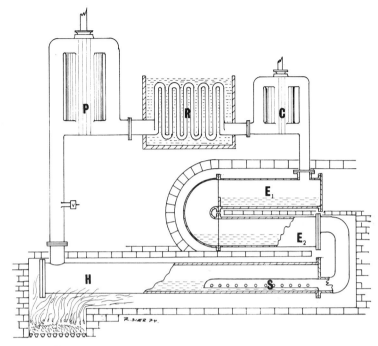

Fig. 3.2 Glazebrook, air engine

nearly as follows, viz:- hydrogen air one hundred, nitrous air one hundred and twenty, carbonic acid one hundred and seventy, atmospheric air two hundred, oxygen five hundred, ammoniac air six hundred and twenty, azottic air six hundred and fifty. Such airs as would act detrimentally on the metals of the machine I use only portions of, according to their purity, for moistening the aforesaid airs or portions of them I make use of water, or other fluids more volatile than water, separately or combined; particularly of such fluids as would of themselves be injurious to the machine I use only in such proportions as their strength will admit without injury to the machine.

His engine might be termed a steam-air engine: the layout is shown diagrammatically in fig. 3.2. The engine was to be fitted with two pistons to be of unequal diameters, C is a double acting air pump fitted with valves as in a steam engine and P is the double acting power cylinder whose diameter was twice that of the air pump, the actual capacity of the air pump being from 20% to 70% of the power cylinder depending on the working fluid being used and the power output required. The two pistons were to be connected to either end of a beam as in a beam engine, or by any other way that would move the pistons 180 deg out of phase. The power cylinder was lagged to reduce heat losses and the air pump cooled. From the air pump air passes into the heater E1 and E2, these heaters having projections from their bottom plates so that one fourth of the internal diameter was filled with water.

From the heaters the air passed into and through what Glazebrook called a saturator, being a pipe immersed in water, with a row of holes along both sides, the air passing through the holes into the hot water, so picking up water vapour. This humid air then passes through H, the final heater. The water level in H and S is maintained at a level equal to one fifth of the internal diameter and is monitored by a float indicator; as the levels fall the float opens a valve allowing a feed pump operated from the beam of the engine to force water into E1 which overflows into E2 thence into H. From H the steam/air passes into the power cylinder, a safety valve being fitted to ensure that the system does not become over-pressurised. The hot gases from the fire are carried in flues so that they pass in turn over S, E1 and E2 before they discharge up the chimney.

A form of regeneration was to be used: the hot air exhausting from the power cylinder could either be discharged into the flues to give up its heat to the incoming cold air from the air pump or, when using gases other than air, could be discharged into a water or air cooled refrigerator R to be used again, the water here being separated and discharged into a hot well supplying the water feed pump, to be used again.

To start the engine the inlet and exhaust valves of the power piston were first opened to allow steam from the heater to pass through, so warming up the machine. After the initial warming up the valves are set closed and the hand air pump A is worked to pressurise the system sufficiently to drive the engine, following which the top inlet valve and bottom exhaust valve are then opened. The piston would then be driven to the bottom of its stroke, so turning the flywheel, which would carry the engine over dead centre. The engine would then pick up speed as the air pump injected air into the system, the speed to be governed by the timing of the inlet valves of the pump, so regulating its delivery. Glazebrook designed his engine to have an operating pressure of between 34 to 49 p.s.i., this to be indicated from a mercury manometer. He also considered using the waste heat from blast furnaces, which is not too surprising considering the number of furnaces that must have been then in use in Coalbrookdale.

By the nature of its construction the steam-air engine showed, at that time, no advantage over the steam engine, but many inventors were to follow with what were claimed improved designs. In 1853 Charles Tetly patented a design for injecting hot water into the hot cylinder to produce a mixture of steam and hot air, and in other designs steam supplied from a separate boiler was injected into the engine. William James' patent of 1864 is typical of this type.

The idea of using a compressor to deliver compressed air at low temperatures into a heating vessel from which it is expanded against a power piston was to feature in many later designs for air engines. George Lilley in a patent granted in 1819 (UK patent 4413) theorised on the advantages:-

> The power obtained by compressing elastic fluids in a certain temperature, and afterwards allowing them to act in a higher temperature, may be made obvious; thus, suppose elastic fluid to be atmospheric air, and that a tube contains 12 cu in with its natural temperature and elasticity, it will require a certain force to compress this air into 2 cu in (say a weight of 13lb falling one foot), but, leaving out the consideration of friction, the elasticity of the air itself (compressed into this compass) would, in the same temperature, raise the same weight to the height whence it fell. If then I place the tube and air in a temperature which would double the elasticity which the same air had in its natural temperature, and then let it expand till it had the same elastic force it had before I compressed it in its natural state, it will give back a force which would raise 26lb a foot high, and have a disposable force of 13lb through the same height; and the same may be said of any other elastic fluid.

Both Lilly and Glazebrook realised the advantages of keeping the compressor cylinder cool. Lilly either surrounded his with a jacket of cold water or circulated a current of cool air around it. The power cylinder was kept hot by the gases from the fire being passed through a jacket surrounding it before passing to the chimney. The power piston was solidly connected to the air compressor and drove the flywheel through a beam, as in a normal beam engine. Both pistons were to be double acting and Lilly fitted rotary valves, driven off the crankshaft by gears, to the power piston instead of the usual slide valve, the air compressor being fitted with simple non-return valves. The compressed air was forced into a reservoir that took the same form as a boiler in a steam engine, placed over a fire, with a capacity of about eight times that of the power cylinder. As in Glazebrook's engine a hand forcing pump was first used to charge the system with compressed air in order to start the engine.

That air could be theoretically more efficient than steam was realised at an early state in the development of the heated air engine, but to realise this in a practical form was to prove more difficult.

In 1818 Petit compared the efficiency of both air and steam engines. He began by proving that the work done in an Isothermal expansion between volumes V1 and V2 was (RT x log V2/V1). This formula he applied to one gramme of water turning to steam, the volume ratio and the latent heat being known; then assuming one gramme of air to absorb the same quantity of heat, its temperature would rise by an amount determined by its specific heat at constant pressure and this was equivalent to a certain volume expansion. It emerged that the air engine was greatly more efficient than the steam engine.

The design of the air engine was also critically examined by another Frenchman, Sadi Carnot. In 1824 Carnot published, in Paris, a small book entitled *Reflections on the motive power of fire and on machines fitted to develop that power* (3). It sold for 3 francs but apparently hardly any one purchased it, although it received one long and excellent review, in the *Revue Encyclopedique*, a journal which covered all branches of literature. In it Carnot established the principle which governs the operation of all heat engines, on the knowledge that when a gaseous fluid is rapidly compressed its temperature rises, and falls when it is rapidly dilated. He invented the closed cycle of operations now known as the Carnot Cycle, that is:-

1. By applying a heat sink A a quantity of air is compressed to volume V with no change of temperature T1.

2. Air is then compressed to volume V2 during which time the temperature rises from T1 to T2.

3. Heat source B at a temperature T2 is then applied and the gas expands from V3 to V2 with no change in temperature.

4. The heat source is then removed, the air is then allowed to expand back to its original volume V1 and the temperature will fall from T2 back to T1.

Carnot reasoned that the effort exerted by the air varies as much by changes in volume as changes in temperature. He noted that for equal volumes or similar positions of the piston of the compressing piston the temperature during compression was less than the temperature during expansion. Since during the latter case the elastic force of the air is found to be greater, the amount of energy produced by expansion is greater than that required to compress the air, so giving an excess

58

power, 'the air then', Carnot stated, 'has served as a heat engine; we have in fact, employed it in the most advantageous manner possible, for no useless re-establishment of equilibrium has been effected by the caloric.'

Finding that the cycle of events was reversible (i.e. could act as a heat pump) Carnot noted that the consumption of motive energy gave rise to a transfer of caloric from B to A equal to the transfer from A to B when producing motive power, this showing the impossibility of a heat engine producing more power than it receives in the form of heat. In theory it would be equal but in practice it will always be less.

Carnot realised that the power developed was dependent on the temperature drop and so established the general proposition:-

The motive power of heat is independent of the agents employed to realise it, its quantity fixed solely by the temperature of the bodies between which it is effected, finally, the transfer of the caloric.

From this we can see that the theoretical efficiency depends only on the limits of the temperature between which an engine works, i.e. $(T1-T2)/T1$. However, Carnot realised this could only take place if there were no direct heat transfer between bodies of different temperatures.

When considering a machine for developing the motive power of heat through the use of elastic fluids (gases or vapours) Carnot laid down the following principles:

1. The temperature of the fluid should be made as high as possible, in order to obtain a great fall of caloric, and consequently a large production of motive power.

2. For the same reason the cooling should be carried as far as possible.

3. It should be so arranged that the passage of the elastic fluid from the highest to the lowest temperature should be due to increase of volume; that is, it should be so arranged that the cooling of the gas should occur as spontaneously as the effect of rarefaction.

4. The limits of the temperature to which it is possible to bring the fluid primarily, are simply the limits of the temperature obtainable by combustion; they are very high.

5. The limits of cooling are found in the temperature of the coldest body of which we can easily and freely make use; this body is usually the water of the locality.

In considering the choice between gas, in the form of atmospheric air, or vapours, in the form of steam, Carnot examined advantages and disadvantages of air:

Plate 4 Sadi Carnot
at the age of 34

1. It presents, as compared with vapour of water, a notable advantage in that, having for equal volume a much less capacity for heat, it would cool more rapidly by an equal increase of volume. (This fact is proved by what has already been stated.) Now we have seen how important it is to produce by change of volume the greatest possible changes of temperature.

2. Vapours of water can be formed only through the intervention of a boiler, while atmospheric air could be heated directly by combustion carried on within its own mass. Considerable loss could be prevented, not only in the quantity of heat, but also in its temperature. This advantage belongs exclusively to atmospheric air. Other gases do not possess it. They would be even more difficult to heat than vapour of water.

3. In order to give to air great increase in volume, and by that expansion to produce a great change of temperature, it must first be taken under a sufficiently high pressure; then it must be compressed with a pump or by some other means before heating it. This operation would require a special apparatus, an apparatus not found in steam-engines. In the latter, water is in a liquid state when injected into the boiler, and to introduce it requires but a small pump.

4. The condensing of the vapour by contact with the refrigerant is much more prompt and much easier than is the cooling of air. There might of course, be the expedient of throwing the latter out of the atmosphere, and there would be also the advantage of avoiding the use of a refrigerant, which is not always available, but it would be requisite that the increase of the volume of the air should not reduce its pressure below that of the atmosphere.

5. One of the gravest inconveniences of steam is that it cannot be used at high temperatures without necessitating the use of vessels of extraordinary strength. It is not so with air for which there exists no necessary relation between the elastic force and the temperature. Air, then, would seem more suitable than steam to realize the motive power of falls of caloric from high temperatures; perhaps at low temperatures steam may be more convenient. We might conceive even the possibility of making the same heat act successively on air and vapour of water. It would be only necessary that the air should have, after its use, an elevated temperature, and instead of throwing it out immediately into the atmosphere, to make it envelop a steam boiler, as if it issued directly from a furnace.

The use of atmospheric air for the development of the motive power of heat presents in practice very great, but perhaps not insurmountable difficulties. If we should succeed in overcoming them, it would doubtless offer a notable advantage over vapour of water.

As to the other permanent gases, they should be absolutely rejected. They have all the inconveniences of atmospheric air, with none of its advantages. The same can be said of other vapours than that of water, as compared with the latter.

In a footnote Carnot examined the working of the 'Pyreolophore' invented by the Niepce cousins, which was a form of explosion engine using the dust of Lycopodium. A more preferable form of working, Carnot thought, would be to compress the air by means of pumps and make it traverse a perfectly closed furnace into which combustible matter had been introduced in small proportions by a mechanism easy of conception, the heated air then acting on a piston to be finally discharged or passed under a steam boiler to utilize the temperature remaining. Carnot saw the main difficulty in enclosing the furnace in a sufficiently strong envelope while ensuring combustion, and to maintain the rest of the engine at a moderate temperature and prevent rapid abrasion of the cylinder and piston, but thought that 'these difficulties do not appear to be insurmountable.' He noted that: 'there have been made, it is said, recently in England, successful attempts to develop motive power through the action of heat on atmospheric air. We are entirely ignorant in what these attempts have consisted – if indeed they have really been made'. At the time of Carnot writing (1824) there had been several experimental engines built in England, though not entirely with success.

4 George Cayley and the furnace gas engine

The furnace gas or gradual combustion engine is not a Hot Air Engine in the accepted use of the word, since power is derived from a combination of heated air and the products of combustion, acting on a piston. However, in the nineteenth century they were classed with the external combustion engine, and their development went hand in hand. The furnace gas engine belongs to a class of engine where fuel is burnt at a constant pressure without explosion. The working pressure is very low and cannot easily be increased, and the speed is also low.

The credit for its development is usually given to Sir George Cayley, though the basic idea pre-dated Cayley, and others like John Ericsson also played their part. Whilst Ericsson soon gave up and went on to develop external combustion engines Cayley persisted and although he spent over fifty years in experimenting he never really perfected his engine, though his basic design is to be found embodied in the many engines that were produced by various manufacturers from about 1860 onwards. Final success lay not with slow speed reciprocating engines but in high speed gas turbines.

Sir George Cayley (1773-1857) is best known today for his pioneering work on heavier-than-air flight. In 1852 he built and successfully flew a glider in which was made the first flight of a fully grown man in a heavier-than-air machine. Cayley could perhaps be described as a technological thinker. As a wealthy landowner of Brompton Hall, Yorkshire, he had the financial independence to work out basic requirements, without looking for immediate cash returns – indeed, he took great pains to publish his works to make the information available free to all and to stop his ideas being patented by others. He is credited with the invention of the caterpillar tractor, the tension wheel, an ink-carrying pen and a self-righting lifeboat. His experiments with the hot air engine seem to have been one of his few failures on which he spent a disproportionate amount of time and energy. From his writings it would appear he could possibly have made the transition from gradual combustion engine to explosion type engine.

In 1809 Cayley wrote:

> It may seem superfluous to inquire further relative to a first mover for aerial navigation, but lightness is of so much value in this instance that it is proper to notice the probability that exists of using the expansion of air, by the sudden expansion combustion of inflammable powders or fluids, with real advantage. The French have lately shown the great power produced by igniting inflammable powders in a closed vessel, and several years ago an engine was made to work in this country in a similar manner by inflammation of spirits of tar. I am not acquainted with the name of the person who invented this engine, but with some minutes with which I was favoured by Mr William Chapman of Newcastle, I find that 30 drops of oil of tar raised 8 cwt to a height of 22in; hence one horsepower could consume from 10 to 12lb per hour, and the engine itself need not exceed 50lb in weight. I am informed by Mr Chapman that this engine was exhibited in a working state to Mr Rennie, but that it was given up in consequence of the expense attending its consumption, being about eight times greater than that of a steam engine of the same power. Probably a much cheaper engine of this sort might be produced by a gas-tight apparatus and firing the inflammable air generated with a due portion of common air under a piston. Upon some of these principles it is perfectly clear that force can be obtained by a much lighter apparatus than the muscles of animals or birds, and therefore in such proportion may aerial vehicles be loaded with inactive matter.

Sir George did make one attempt, though not a successful one, to construct a small engine for some experiments on the force of gunpowder and the heat evolved by its explosion acting on a quantity of air. In his notes he recorded that he used gunpowder for generating heat in a 'very odd sort of boiler'. He admitted that, although he had never suffered an accident in the course of his experiments, he never liked to venture near the boiler when turning the engine. On the possibility of using gunpowder for motive power he later commented, 'who would take the double risk of breaking their necks or being blown to atoms?'

Cayley first considered the use of heated air some time about 1799 as shown by a memorandum which is unfortunately unsigned but is not written in Sir George's hand.

> I hereby acknowledge that the following principle for the construction of a steam engine was first communicated to me by Sir George Cayley on the 2 day of Nov 1799 upon the promise of my not making use of the principle with-out his concent; namely the application of steam or heated air to drive out any heavy fluid in which a hollow drum turning on an axis shall be immersed in such a manner that one side of the drum shall constantly be filled with steam or air and the other filled with heavy fluid which action is performed a vacuum (or as near an approach to one as can be effected) to be made above the surface of such heavy fluid as may be used.

The device described seems to be very similar to the one proposed by Amontons in 1699, but there is no indication that it was ever built. He did however go on to build an experimental engine of the piston type, the design of which he published some years later in 1807 (1). To achieve power output two pistons of unequal diameters were used, one acting as a feed pump and the other as the power piston, in much the same way as had Glazebrook (1797 and 1801). The following is Cayley's description of his engine (fig. 4.1).

To Mr. Nicholson.
Sir.   Brompton, Sept. 25, 1807.
I observed in your last vol. p. 368 that some experiments have been lately made in France upon air, expanded by heat, applied as a first mover for mechanical purposes. This idea, as you justly remark, is by no means new in this country; yet I have not yet heard that any

Plate 5 George Cayley

Fig. 4.1 Cayley, air engine (c.1800)

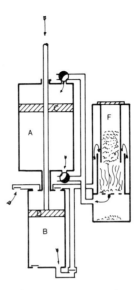

successful experiments have been made, exclusively upon this principle, in England, though you hint that something promising has been accomplished relative to it. The subject is of much importance as the steam engine has hitherto proved too weighty and cumbrous for most purposes of locomotion; whereas the expansion of air seems calculated to supply a mover free from these defects. Under this impression I send to you a sketch of an engine I projected upon this principle several years ago; it was made on a considerable scale at Newcastle, though I must confess without success in the result, which I attributed to the imperfect manner in which it was executed, the cylinders being made of sheet copper and so irregular, as not to be rendered tolerably air-tight by any packing of the piston. I think that there can be no doubt that the scheme is practicable in some way or other; and I conceive that the form of the engine here sketched will be the basis of whatever experience may prove to perfection in the apparatus of the air engine.

A and B, pl. VIII fig 1, are two cylinders, placed one above the other; C and D, their respective pistons connected by one rod. F is a cylinder, containing a fire in a vessel within a vessel within it in such a manner, that any air passing between the upper and lower portions of it must go through the fire. This vessel also contains a long cylinder, open at the bottom, and directly over the centre of the fire, for the purpose of holding coke or other fuel. This cylinder is

65

covered at the top, and packed air-tight when it has served the purpose of permitting the fire to be kindled through it: and has been filled with fuel.

The cylinder B is fitted up to answer the purpose of a double stroke forcing pump, or bellows, to drive the air into the upper portion of vessel F, from whence it passes downward through the fire for the purpose of consuming the smoke (the fresh fuel being supplied from the reservoir above) in its passage through the more completely ignited cinders below. In this act the air is expanded; and by means of pipes from the lower portion of F, it is conveyed alternately above and below the piston of the cylinder A. In each pipe is fixed a stop cock or valve, so constructed as to open a passage to the external air, when it shuts the connection with the fire vessel. These cocks are worked by a plug frame.

From this construction it will appear evident that whatever expansion the air receives its pressure will operate alike upon the piston of the bellows and of the receiver; and that always in opposition to each other; hence the power of the stroke will be in proportion to the excess of the area of the receiving piston, over that of the feeding one, multiplied by the expansive force of the contained air, and by the length of the movement.

If when the engine is well constructed, the expansion of the air in keeping up the fire be not found sufficiently sensible, still the form of the engine is such as to admit of either inflammable gas, oil of tar, or some other inflammable matters, being injected each stroke upon the fire; so that all the heat generated by the united combustion may operate without waste; perhaps even a light sprinkling of water, either upon, or round the sides of the fire, might answer the purpose. It scarcely need be observed, that a tube connected with a small forcing pump are the only things required for producing these effects.

I remain Sir,
Your obedient Servant,
GEORGE CAYLEY.

The experimental engine described was built by the Newcastle firm of William Chapman to a design drawn up by Cayley. His early work did not pass unnoticed, for in a patent granted in 1816 to Montgolfier the following comment was made: 'I do hereby declare that we do not make claim to the invention of the furnace with an interior fire, nor to such parts of the machine as are marked with the letters of the alphabet in the drawings the same having been practised before by Sir George

Cayley' (See Chapter One).

Several patents were granted for engines that used an enclosed fire through which air was passed, in addition to Montgolfier's patent mentioned above.

In 1821 a patent was granted to Robert Stein (UK patent 4537) for an engine to be worked on a mixture of steam and hot air. Coal was to be fed into a closed ash-pit by a fluted roller, and another fluted roller was employed for withdrawing the ashes from the ash-pit. Air was forced into the furnace by a pump and the products of combustion generated steam in a boiler to be used in conjunction with the air to work the engine.

A patent was granted in 1821 to Neil Arnott (UK patent 4615) for 'Improvements connected with the Production and Agency of Heat in Furnaces, Steam and Air Engines, Distilling, evaporating and brewing apparatus', in which among other things he describes an internal combustion engine.

The engine was intended to be operated at a temperature of between 500-600°F and was to be constructed of closed chamber containing the furnace, two double acting cylinders, one double the capacity of the other, the smaller forming an air pump that forced air up through the grate of the fire, into the heating chamber. Self-acting valves were to be fitted to the air pump and hot air admission to the power cylinder controlled by an elaborate rotary valve actuated intermittently from the flywheel such that the valve was stepped round ¼ revolution at a time. The two cylinders were to be in the form of a U with the lower part filled with oil. The piston was to work in one leg of the U within the oil, the air acting on the surface of the oil in each leg. This arrangement Arnott claimed 'will obviate the necessity of fine workmanship or fitting; but if the apparatus is well made it will act without this, and may be made of smaller capacity'.

Arnott also described a piston engine (fig. 4.2):

If we suppose a fire to be placed on a grate near the bottom of a closed cylinder d, o and the cylinder to be filled of fresh air recently admitted and if we suppose the loose piston g, d to be pulled upwards it is evident that all the air in the cylinder above d will be made to pass by the tube through the fire and will receive an increased elasticity according to the expansion or increase in volume which the fire is capable of giving it. If these were only single close vessels then the expansion might be so strong as to burst it, but if another vessel be of equal size were to be provided communicating with the first through the passage b and containing a close fitting

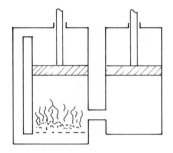

Fig. 4.2 Arnott, air engine (1828)

piston e, f like that of a steam engine the expansion of the air in the first would act to lift the said piston, and so might work a water pump, or do any other service which a steam engine can perform. At the end of the lifting stroke of the piston f, c it might be made to operate a escape valve for the hot air, placed in any convenient part of the apparatus and to cause the descent of the blowing piston d to expel that air. While a new supply of fresh air would enter above d. The engine would then be ready to repeat its stroke as before, and the working would be continued as in a steam engine.

The main problems in operating this form of engine, Arnott thought, would be in overheating and destruction of the valves by dust (21).

In 1826 a patent was granted to John Ericsson for an engine to be worked by the products of combustion. An air pump was used to force air into an enclosed furnace and the air was made to act on a piston or used to produce steam. The design is more fully described in Chapter Six.

In 1828 a patent was granted to Samuel Hall (UK patent 5659) for an engine to be powered by the products of combustion and steam. The engine was to have pistons of unequal diameters and an enclosed fire.

Although his early experiments were a failure Cayley's interest was renewed through his close association with Goldsworthy Gurney. Gurney had built and operated steam carriages and in 1829 drove one from London to Bath. Cayley had been instrumental in trying to get the Turnpike Acts repealed and a steam carriage bill through Parliament, though without success, to the detriment of steam transport. Sir George's mechanic, Tom Wadeson, was closely involved in the building of Sir Goldsworthy's steam carriages and was to be killed in an accident while driving one in 1840. Cayley was also associated with Dr William Harland of Scarborough who patented, in 1827, a steam carriage and also built a working model. Harland and Cayley, it seems, between them 'kept an excellent mechanic continually at work' (4). In a letter he sent to Gurney in 1853 Cayley wrote: 'My attention as you so justly observe, was directed entirely to such application of air, as would suit loco-motive purposes, having your old crochet of turnpike road movement in view, as certainly practicable, and aerial navigation as that which the air engine in its finally improved condition would sooner or later redeem in all human probability.'

Cayley designed his engines on the principle that air doubles in volume at a temperature of 480°F and he sought to heat the air to a temperature of 520°F on passing through the fire. A series of experiments was carried out in 1826 using a pair of bellows, one being exactly double the size of the other, and was intended to show the results of expansion and also consumption of fuel. One of the main problems to be overcome was that the slide valves used in the early engine were torn to pieces in a short time by the heat and dust, which also damaged the piston: this problem was overcome by using conical valves. An experimental engine of 1hp was built at Brompton Hall and seems to have worked reasonably well. The cold piston was 10.5in in diameter and the hot piston 13.5in, with the stroke of both being 12in. The fireplace was 10in in diameter by 11in deep in a generator containing 20 cu ft of air. The head of pressure, taken by mercurial gauge, was 8 to 9lb and the engine ran at 90 rpm (2). Conical valves were used and the hot cylinder was made of copper, the power output being found on a friction brake and by pumping water.

A second experimental engine was built in London, but was not so successful and was taken to Brompton to be worked on. It seems that on one occasion the engine gave out 20.5hp but when working with the throttle nine-tenths shut 6hp was maintained, with the piston travelling

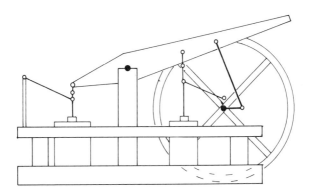

Fig. 4.3 Cayley, Brompton engine (1832)

with a velocity of 252 ft/min, the fuel consumption being 5lb of coke/hp/hr.

Fig. 4.3 shows the general arrangement of the engine that Cayley erected in the Brew House at Brompton.

In a patent granted in 1837 (UK patent 7351) Sir George embodied all the improvements he had made in his engine. It is interesting to note that the patent was for 'Certain improvements in the apparatus for propelling carriages on common roads or railways part of which improvements may be applied to other useful purposes'. Over the years Cayley had tried to help his friend Gurney with his steam carriage and Gurney had done all he could to help iron out problems in the air engine. Gurney made a number of experiments himself, especially to prevent leakage of air under pressure between the cylinder and piston (3). In 1837 Cayley drew up an agreement with Gurney to share with him any profits that might have been made from the air engine in return for his 'valuable co-operation in bringing my invention (now only exhibiting its powers in an experimental engine) into the most efficient and convenient form'.

The layout of the engine described in the patent follows the lines of his experimental engine except that it is inverted so that it could drive the wheel of a carriage.

To enable the power output of his engine to be controllable he devised a special furnace (fig. 4.4) the outer casing of which was constructed of sheet iron with detachable covers top and bottom, to

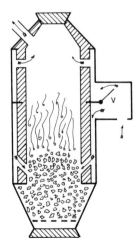

Fig. 4.4 Cayley, improved furnace (1832)

enable the removal of ashes from the grate. Within this was contained, leaving a space all around for the passage of air from the pump, an inner lining of firebricks that contained the fire. The space between the firebox and outer casing was split into two compartments forming upper and lower air boxes, communicating with the fire by passages in the firebricks. By means of a flap valve V the air from the air pump could be directed into the upper or lower air boxes. By this means air could be directed above or below the fire, so diminishing or increasing the intensity of the fire, by varying the amount of air passing through it. Fuel was supplied to the fire from a separate airtight hopper. In the improved power piston, to reduce the effect of hot gases destroying the piston a drum or plunger was placed on top of the piston to act as a heat shield, its diameter being slightly less than that of the cylinder, the idea being that the plunger was surrounded by a thin film of air that would further inhibit heat conduction. An attempt to reduce the abrasive action was made by filtering the air before it entered the power cylinder by means of an ash separator made up from one or more layers of fine wire mesh.

When first used the heat shield was, in length, about equal to half the stroke of the piston but this was later extended to rather more than the length of stroke for better effect. In his patent Cayley recommends that the portion of the cylinder in which the piston moves be cooled by means of a water jacket whilst the upper part be insulated to reduce the heat losses, and suggests that the hot exhaust gases could be used to preheat the cold air from the air pump before entering the fire, though there is no evidence that Cayley used either. To start the engine and to provide surges of power when required water was to be sprinkled over the fire to produce steam. Cayley's claim to priority for the improved furnace seems to have caused some concern, as in 1837 Gurney wrote to Sir George to say that he had been studying Ericsson's patent and pointed out that Ericsson had said 'I lay no claim to the invention of forcing air in, under and over the fire', which, commented Gurney, 'Make me suspect they have seen your paper. On the whole without further remark, he will not interfere with you, tho' he is very close upon you'. However, an examination of Ericsson's 1829 patent (no. 5763) for improvements in steam boilers clearly shows regulation of the fire by blowing air under or over the fire and in the patent the claim was made '. . . the fuel is supplied with air both above and below, as shown in the drawing annexed, which double supply of air, regulated by cocks as afore said, we claim as new; . . .' and in the text the air cocks are indicated '. . . three air cocks to admit atmospheric air to the top of the fuel in the furnace J; an air cock to admit atmospheric air to the bottom of the said fuel; . . .'. Ericsson used his forced draught boiler in his railway engine the *Novelty*, which was entered in the Rainhill trials, the merits of which were discussed in the pages of the *Mechanics Magazine* for 24th October and 5th December 1829.

For all his efforts Sir George never really achieved real success with his engine. His problems are summed up in a letter he wrote to Charles Babbage in 1853:

> I made several experimental engines; and the first that succeeded, a one horse power, made entirely under my own direction here at Brompton worked for days together without inconvenience from dust or heat. When I got to London my plans were over-ruled by the fancied superiority of London workmanship, and the engine proved more faulty than before, such experimental engines, as you well know, are costly matters; and our funds are exhausted, and the shop taken from us for other purposes, before the engine had a fair chance of being freed from its remaining evils. I am now making one myself again and I hope to get quit of the evils of dirt, or over-heated piston. I am now 79 and in tolerable force for an old fellow.

Robert Stirling had his ideas put into practice by his brother James who had access to the machine shop of the foundry he was manager of and John Ericsson never seemed to have trouble in raising funds for his many experiments , but Cayley it seemed paid for his experimenting out of his own pocket and so was never able to achieve in practice what he felt in theory to be right.

It is clear that what Sir George sought was a lighter, safer alternative to the steam engine. In 1839 he wrote to John Marshall, a director of the Leeds railway, to suggest the use of his air engine on railways:

> . . . the engine is, however, necessarily bulky though not necessarily heavy, but I think for railroad purposes we ought not to exceed 12 horse power, and as I expect the engine will be much cheaper and much more durable (for indeed I do not see what is to wear out but what can readily and cheaply be renewed) I think it will be best to run smaller trains and more of them – which would have many advantages. It would save the terrible wear on the rails and wheels and accommodate the public with half-hour trains. You know the merits of the air engine and the faults, heavy one, of the present system.

In reply to a letter received from Robert Taylor, Cayley wrote:

> . . . two horse power is required to effect the flight of one man and

steam is too heavy within the weight required; hence I have been at work within the last 30 years at many sorts of first movers of a lighter description, and have constructed several engines worked by the expansion of air by heat. They were made as experimental engines only, and were not constructed lightly at all, but to work out the problems of using air in lieu of water. Two year ago I showed one of these at work to Messrs. Babbage, Rennie, Renson etc., all being the first judges of mechanical matter. They tested it to be a five and quarter horse power, and the only weight of food it required was 6 pounds of coke per horse power, the same steam power would have required 70lb of water and coke per hour. There were some faults in that engine but its power was undoubted, and I am now endeavouring to make one to correct these faults. If I can realise my plans in the air engine, or some one will invent a lighter, mechanical navigation is in hand at once.

In spite of all the setbacks Cayley persisted with his engine. In a letter written in 1853 he stated 'I am now very busy making an air engine of 5 horse power' and in 1852 he sketched a design for an engine on 'Ericsson's principle' and is 'for merely experimental purpose of a model flying machine'. In another notebook he wrote in 1854:

With a view to making a small power engine for model artificial inclined plane aerial navigation, I considered that spirits of wine offers several convenient properties. It can be burnt without any furnace, in a small space, the supply may be stroke by stroke, and only as many charges given as the experiment in hand may require. One pound of spirits of wine will melt 60 pounds of ice at 32 deg F . . .

The use of alcohol as a fuel would seem to indicate that he was leading up to designing an explosive type internal combustion engine.

Sir George Cayley died in Brompton Hall only 12 days short of his 84th birthday, too soon to see the air engine, that he had put so much effort into perfecting, go into general use. Over the next thirty years furnace gas engines were made not only in Britain but also in America and Europe. An interesting adaptation of the closed furnace was proposed by Alexander Gordon, who having examined Cayley's Mill-bank engine and witnessed the engines of Stirling and Ericsson, drew up a design for propelling boats by the direct application of the products of combustion, without the intervention of any machinery between the furnace and the water to be acted upon by the hot blast. He called his machine a 'Fumic Impeller' and was granted a patent in 1845 (UK patent 10,544).

The boat with which Gordon experimented was 26ft long and 4½ft broad, weighing 4375lb. The propelling apparatus consisted of a closed furnace with openings top and bottom, to allow the fire to be got up to the required temperature, when they were then closed off. Air was supplied by a common small forge bellows working only on the down stroke, giving a blast of air which was sent to the bottom of the furnace to then pass up through the fire. A 3in pipe led from the top of the furnace to the stern of the boat to discharge at a point 12in below the surface of the water.

It was found that the first blast by one man always started the boat from a state of rest, 3ft in two seconds. Gordon thought that 'no two men, with oars, or sculls, with all the advantage of their flexor and extensor muscles, could do more. And neither paddle-wheels, nor the Archimedean screw, can start the same weight into such motion in the same time'.

In 1856, the Novelty Ironworks, in New York, U.S.A., built a large railway locomotive called the *Vampire*, which weighed 44 tons and cost $4000, for parties in Saint Louis. It was intended to be propelled by the products of combustion, mingled with steam from water injected into the fire, and also steam made by a water-jacket surrounding the fire. This hot mixture was first conveyed around the cylinder, then into it, and after being exhausted, gave up its heat to the incoming air. The locomotive, the invention of which was attributed to one P. Bennet, was tried on the Erie Railway, near Paterson, and succeeded in running itself into a ditch, after making a mile and a half at the rate of twelve miles per hour. The cylinders, cut by the ashes, had to be rebored and the engine refitted once or twice, but the project was a total failure.

One of the early successful stationary engines was the Roper built by the Roper Caloric Engine Company of New York, U.S.A. (5). These engines were made in four sizes, 9in cylinder and 9in stroke, ½hp; 12in cylinder and 12in stroke, 1hp; 16in cylinder and 16in stroke, 3hp; 18in cylinder and 18in stroke, 4hp (6). Test results from an engine loaded on a Prony brake show that an engine with 16in piston with 16in stroke and air pump with 13in piston and 17½in stroke gave 2.572bhp at 85rpm. An engine with 18in piston and 16in stroke with air pump 15in piston and 16in stroke gave 5.15ihp at 85rpm.

The design was patented in 1863 (UK patent 155, 1863), and fig. 4.5 shows the general layout of the engine. P is the power piston with A the air pump, the air being passed above or below the fire. V1 and V2 are simple flap valves, V3 the inlet valve to the power cylinder and V4 the exhaust valve, both driven from the crankshaft CS.

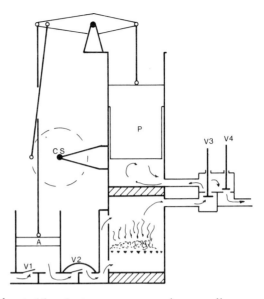

Fig. 4.5 Roper, air engine (1863)

The Roper took about 15 minutes to start and normally ran at between 80 and 90rpm. An engine of this design was built in England by Edwards & Co in the late 1860s. During a lecture on Wenham's engine held in 1873, Mr E. J. C. Welsh made the following observations on experiments he had made with Edwards' engine in 1867. One of the chief difficulties he had met was the distortion of the working parts from the engine getting too hot; the longer it worked, the hotter it became and the working parts got out of square, causing friction enough to stop the engine. The lubrication of the piston had been a source of trouble, the packing being made simply with three ordinary rings; plumbago alone was first tried, and then a mixture of plumbago and soapstone, which was found to lubricate more efficiently than plumbago alone. When the engine got too hot, leakage arose, and a very slight leakage of the air was sufficient to bring the engine to a standstill, nor did there seem to be any means of supplying an extra large air pump sufficiently to compensate for these ordinary leakages. The door of the furnace was ground on its seat, and every precaution taken to prevent leakage, but without success. Another difficulty had been that particles from the ashes carried over from the furnace got under the air valves and prevented them from closing completely; anything that caused the valves to stick was of course fatal to the working of the engine, and he tried equilibrium slide valves instead of the flap valves and found it worked satisfactorily. Welsh had an engine made with a cylinder of only 6in diameter and with a separate pump to maintain the supply of compressed air, but though carefully made the friction in so small an engine was found to absorb all the power that could be generated.

The following is an advertisement placed in the *English Mechanic* for 21st September 1866.

HEATED AIR ENGINE

For all small purposes, such as driving Printing Presses and Lathes, hoisting, pumping, and for agricultural uses, the above Engine is the cheapest that can be found.

It can run for 10 hours a day, for an expence of from five to six shillings a week, reckoning coals at thirty shillings a ton. It needs no engineer, and twenty minutes attention suffices to run it a day. No water being used all danger of an explosion is done away with. For further particulars apply to

W. Y. EDWARDS AND CO.,
7, CASTLE STREET, FALCON SQUARE, CITY, LONDON.

In the 22nd June 1866 issue of the *English Mechanic* a description was given of the new engine. It was claimed that some hundreds were in use in America, driving shoe machinery, printing presses, saws, machinery, hoisting, pumping, turning, meat cutting, &c, &c. Edwards and Co were described as agents for London.

The dimensions for a nominal 2hp engine were given as pump 12in diameter and power piston 16in, consumption of anthracite coal as 8lb per hour, space occupied given as 6ft square.

In his patent (no. 2190, 1868) James Churchill gives his address as Oxford Street, and in an 1868 advert Edwards & Co gave 531 Oxford Street, London as their address.

Churchill's patent was for improvements in the construction of the working cylinder and piston and also for the formation of air passages in the bed plate, otherwise the general layout of the engine detailed in the patent drawing seems to follow closely that of the Roper engine.

These engines were not, it seems, without their problems, as shown by the following reader's query that appeared in the 5th August 1881 copy of the *English Mechanic and World of Science*.

I have come into possession of a hot air engine, known as Churchill's patent, and sold by Edwards and Co, 531 Oxford Street. It worked well with the previous owner but by some accident it got overheated and the valves were warped. They were sent to a machinist at

Manchester, and apparently put right, but it has never gone since. No one here seems to understand it, and the seller has left Oxford Street. If any of our Readers can give information on the subject, it will be much esteemed, and I would send any further particulars – Chemicus, Dewsbury.

The Exeter and Bristol Railway purchased seven engines from Fox, Walker and Co in 1868-70, which were used to drive three throw pumps by belt drive and were capable of delivering 2000 gallons an hour when running at 72rpm and consumed a bucket full of anthracite every two hours. One engine worked at Chard until 1937. This engine was examined by the author and found to stand some 7ft high, the air pump piston having a diameter of 13½in and stroke of 9¾in. The power piston has a stroke of 8in with a diameter of 18½in, the flywheel being some 5ft 4½in in diameter.

Another engine of American design was that by Philander Shaw (UK patent 2797, 1861). His engine was awarded a gold medal in 1865 by the Mechanics Association of Massachusetts, who stated that 'this engine contains more of new and meritorious invention than any other machine that has come to our notice'. Shaw built an engine for the Paris Exposition Universelle of 1867 of which *The Engineer* said:

Amongst the host of engines and the forest of machinery now collected in the Champs de Mars, calling forth our admiration and astonishment at the general perfection of design and workmanship, but for the most part wanting in that more attractive feature, novelty, it is quite refreshing to find ourselves opposite an engine to which the palm of originality in many essential respects cannot be denied. Such is Mr Philander Shaw's air engine. Cramped in its design and inferior in its workmanship, it is still, perhaps, the most interesting machine in the exhibition, to those, at least, of our readers who are interested in prime movers, whether they believe in the ultimate possibility of employing hot air instead of steam in large engines or not (10).

The engine ran an average of over 20hp for a consumption of 1.4lb of coal per hp hour.

The engine had two vertical single acting cylinders with trunk piston; fig. 4.6 shows the general layout of cylinders and piston. The cylinders were 24in in diameter and that of the trunks 15½in, the piston having an 18in stroke. The effect of using trunk pistons was to give the piston an effective area below the piston greater than that above, the upper side acting as the air pump and that below the power piston. A form of

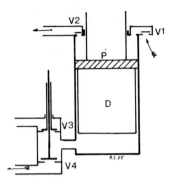

Fig. 4.6 Shaw, air engine (1861)

regeneration was used; on the downward stroke air was drawn in above the piston and on the up stroke the air was forced into the furnace at 15psi. First the cold air was passed through a casing around the main valves, so keeping them cool, and the air was then passed through a heat exchanger consisting of multi tubes where it was heated by the hot gases exhausted from under the piston; the warmed air then passed into the furnace above and below the fire. The inlet and outlet valves V3 and V4 were moved by cams, the inlet valve being open for ⅚ths of the upstroke. To protect the piston a hollow drum D was fitted beneath the piston P of slightly smaller diameter, and an attempt to keep hot gases and grit away from the polished part of the cylinder wall was made; at the moment that the piston was to make its up stroke, but before the main valve had opened, a jet of cold air was forced into the annular space at a pressure equal to that of the incoming hot gases so it was hoped keeping out the hot smoky gases. At the exhibition the pistons did not become overheated.

In a patent taken out in 1868 (UK patent 3804) by Lars Albert Leonard Sonderstrom a trunk piston is also used, also the cold air from the pump was preheated by the exhausting hot gases.

Another single piston design is found in patents taken out in 1867 by F. H. Wenham. Wenham, an aeronautical pioneer, was one of the founders of the Aeronautical Society of Great Britain. His engine was single acting with one cylinder, and to enable a single piston to have two functions the cylinder length was such that at the top of the stroke the piston did not reach the cylinder cover but left a considerable clearance between them. This clearance was so arranged that the air was compressed to half its volume, giving 15psi at constant temperature, which was found, by experiment, to be the best practical working pressure.

Fig. 4.7 Wenham,
air engine (1867)

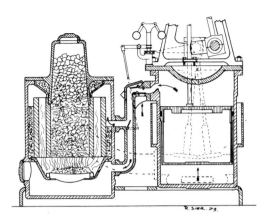

Fig. 4.7 shows the general layout. In fig. 4.8A is shown an indicator diagram taken from an engine of 3hp, at a time it was doing full duty on a frictional brake; the engine had a cylinder of 24in diameter with 12in stroke and running at 108rpm with a mean effective pressure of 11.2lb. Fig. 4.8B shows the indicator diagram of the air pump, and represents the power required for compressing the air above the piston. In this diagram it can be seen that the line begins from the zero point on the left of the diagram, and gradually rises with the usual compression curve till it arrives a little beyond half stroke; during this time the delivery valve is not open, and no air is sent into the furnace. The mean pressure as shown by the dotted line is 4.6lb.

As soon as the pressure of the air in the pump begin to exceed that of the furnace, the delivery valve rises, and during the remainder of the stroke the compressed air is delivered from the pump into the furnace. When the piston arrives at the top of its stroke, the delivery valve closes; when the piston begins to descend there is a pressure of 15psi above it

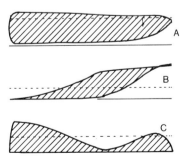

Fig. 4.8 Wenham air
engine indicator diagrams

79

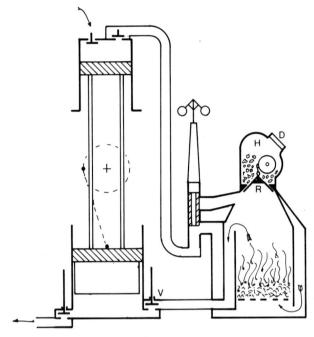

Fig. 4.9 Bucket, air engine (1863)

and with the body of compressed air being confined into a space considerable capacity exerts a gradually diminishing force to about half stroke. In calculating therefore the force required to compress the air, this down stroke has to be deducted in the measurement of the diagram. The difference between the mean pressure in the pump (as shown in fig. B) and the mean driving pressure below the piston as shown in fig. 4.8B is 6.6psi, which represents the effective driving pressure as shown in the combined indicator diagram fig. 4.8C. From the fact of the engine being single acting with a large cylinder, the friction, as might be expected, is great compared to the power, for it is found that while the indicated horse power, as shown by the combined diagram, amounts to 9.76 the actual working power obtained at the friction brake amounts to only 3.30hp.

Wenham found that his engine ran best on inferior bituminous coal, particularly if of high moisture content. Dry plumbago powder was found to be the best lubricant for the cylinder, and as with all engines of this type it was found that the slightest of air leaks was sufficient to bring the engine to a halt (12). From experiments with an electrical pyrometer it was found that the air entered the working cylinder at a temperature of 1127°F and was exhausted at a temperature of 446°F, so that nearly 40% of the whole heat was thrown away in the exhaust. The engines were made in three sizes: 12in (½hp); 15in and 24in (4hp).

In 1871 patents were taken out by A. K. Rider for what were modifications to Ericsson's engines to give working with internal combustion.

In a design by J. Bucket (UK patent 4413, 1863 and 2075, 1876) the problem of heat damage to the valves was overcome by first passing

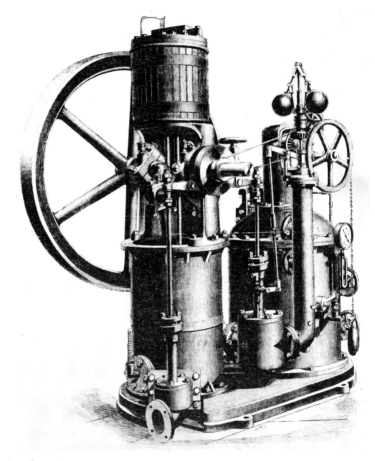

Plate 6 Bucket engine

81

cold air from the air pump around the valve casing, so preventing overheating (6, 7). Fig. 4.9 gives a diagrammatic layout of Bucket's engine. V is the valve that is cooled. The upper cylinder acts as the air pump and coal is fed into the furnace through the hopper H and the door D. During this time the valve R closes the top, to maintain the air pressure in the furnace during stoking. By opening the cock a portion of the air enters the hopper, and the air pressure is equalised. As soon as D is closed R is lowered into the furnace by the chain S. Speed was controlled by a governor that regulated combustion by passing air above or below the fire. These engines were built by the Caloric Engine Co and made as either single cylinder or double cylinder, where the cranks were placed at right angles.

In a trial of a double cylinder engine, of 12hp, some of the deficiencies of this class of engine are well shown.

The gross ihp was 42.24 and the pump ihp was 21.04, thus half the power was employed in negative work leaving only 21.20hp for working the engine. The bhp was 14.39 giving a mechanical efficiency of only 71%. The mean pressure on the pistons was 18.5lb, and on the pumps 16.78psi. The coke consumption was 2.54lb per bhp per hr and only about 8% of the total heat supplied was converted into work. The engine ran at 61rpm and the diameter of the working piston was 24in and that of the pump was 18in with the stroke being 16in for both. Fig. 4.10 shows an indicator diagram taken from the engine, from which the mean effective pressure was found to be 18⅓psi.

A similar design was built for the Northern Lights Commissioners, for use on lightships, by the Pulsometer Engine Co of Nine Elms, London. They were used for generating compressed air for use in fog sirens. These engines were a nominal 6hp with a motor cylinder of 24in and air pump of 18in, both of 18in stroke (8).

Engines built by A. & F. Brown of New York, USA, were also used in lighthouses. At the South Foreland lighthouse, 10hp engines running at 60rpm were used to drive dynamos to give a light of 3620 candlepower. Each engine drove two dymamos running at 850rpm (9).

In all the engines so far examined the fuel is burnt in a vessel separate to the cylinders. In 1827 John Ericsson had experimented with an engine where the fire was placed at the bottom of one cylinder, but

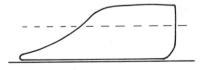

Fig. 4.10 Bucket, air engine indicator diagram.

his experiments were not a success and he turned to the external air engine. Placing the fire within the cylinder reduces the amount of fuel that can be burnt, necessitating some form of continual fuel feed.

In an engine of American design, invented by C. C. Leavitt (fig. 4.11), the coal is placed in the hemispherical receptacle, a semi-circular feed bar oscillates on a pivot, and at each movement raises on its inner end a small supply of coal. A wire brush, which has a horizontal movement, brushes off the coal thus raised into the open mouth of the coke or grate, the latter being so constructed that it completely closes the passage of the firebox, both when receiving the coal and when delivering it into the cylindrical passage in front of the plunger. The plunger is operated by an arm linked to the rod. When the firebox is full the plunger meets so much resistance that it cannot move. This causes the belt to slip on the pulleys, so feeding stops.

The engine was a small one with 6in pistons with 6in stroke set at 90 deg, the power piston in advance of the pump, and it ran at 150rpm. When the hot or power piston was at the top of its stroke the exhaust valve V3 opened and the hot piston on descending exhausted the hot gases. The cold piston began to rise when the hot piston was halfway down its stroke, mixing cold air with the exhausting gases and so preventing damage to the valve. Cold clean air passes lastly through the valve, so freeing the valve seat of grit and ensuring its complete closure.

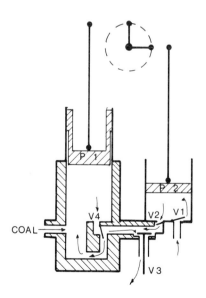

Fig. 4.11 Leavitt,
air engine

83

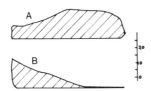

Fig. 4.12 Leavitt air engine indicator diagrams

This occurs a little before the end of the travel of the hot piston P1 and mid-stroke of the pump P2. As the pump piston is moving faster than the hot piston there is some compression of the air. Fig. 4.12 gives indicator diagrams taken from the cylinders: in the air pump, diagram B, the atmospheric line on the right is when the air is being discharged to waste. The engine developed 0.27ihp for fuel consumption of 4.63lb of coal per hour (13).

In a design by Benier (14) the two cylinders were placed at right angles and a common crank drove the horizontal air pump, via a rocking lever, and the vertical power cylinder via a beam (fig. 4.13). Air

Plate 7   Benier engine

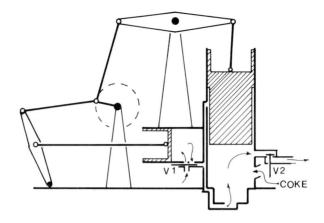

Fig. 4.13 Benier, air engine

from the air pump was fed in above and below the fire, which was set
directly below the power cylinder. Some of the cold air was bled off and
pumped in below the hot piston, between the drum and the cylinder
wall, thus keeping the dust and grit away from the piston sliding surface.
Air to and from the pumping cylinder was controlled by a slide valve V1.
Small pieces of coke were automatically fed into the fire which was set
below the hot piston, though in practice it was found that the feeding
device could be jammed if too large lumps of coke were used. V2 is the
exhaust valve.

An engine was fully tested by Professor Slaby at Cologne in December 1887. The engine examined was a nominal 4hp, with an air pump of
279.5mm diameter and 225.5mm stroke. The power or hot piston was
339.8mm diameter and 349.5mm stroke. At a speed of 117rpm the total

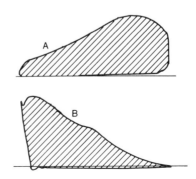

Fig. 4.14 Benier air
engine indicator diagrams

85

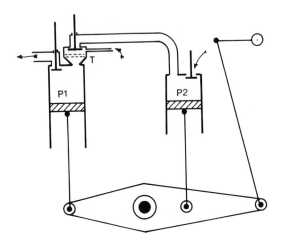

Fig. 4.15 Brayton Ready Motor

indicated work in the power cylinder was 9.23hp and in the air pump 3.38hp, leaving only 5.85hp available for useful work. On the friction brake the power was 4.03, which gives a mechanical efficiency of 69%. The fuel consumption was 3.6lb per bhp or 3.1lb per 1hp, only 6% of the total heat supplied being turned into useful work (15, 16). Fig. 4.14 shows the indicator diagrams that were obtained. These engines were built in the following sizes – 4hp, 6hp, 9hp, 12hp, 15hp, 20hp – and were used in French lighthouses, the builders being the Cie Francaise des Moteurs a Air Chaud, Paris.

In all the engines so far discussed the fuel, in the form of coal or some other solid fuel, is burnt continuously during the power stroke. An engine that burnt a liquid fuel was Brayton's 'Ready Motor', designed in America by George Brady Brayton (1839-92) and patented by him (UK patents 432, 1872; 2209, 1874 and 11062, 1890). It is interesting to note that *The Engineer* described it as a hydro-carbon hot air engine and compared it to those of Cayley and Wenham (17). Brayton's first venture was for an engine using gas but problems with this led him to use oil as a fuel in the next two patents, though the design was basically the same (18). The engines (fig. 4.15) had two cylinders of equal diameters but unequal strokes, the two pistons P1 and P2 being connected to either end of a beam. Air from the air pump was compressed into an air receiver at about 60 to 80psi. From the receiver air was mixed with the fuel and passed into the power cylinder via a flame trap T. An inlet valve cut off the fuel after the piston valve had

Fig. 4.16 Brayton
Ready Motor indicator
diagrams

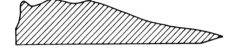

travelled about 40% of its stroke and at about 90% of stroke the exhaust valve opened. To provide ignition a small amount of air fuel mixture was continuously passed into the cylinder to provide a pilot flame, and as the pressure in the receiver was always greater than that in the power cylinder the flame could not be snuffed out. Ignited by the pilot flame, the air fuel mixture entered the cylinder as a continuous flame, the flame trap preventing flame-back into the air receiver.

A Brayton engine was extensively tested by Dugald Clerk, in 1878 at the Crown Iron Works, Glasgow (19). The engine was made by the New York and New Jersey Ready Motor Co. The motor cylinder was 8in in diameter and the stroke was 12in; the pump cylinder was also 8in in diameter, and the stroke 6in. A brake was applied to the flywheel, fully loading the engine. The result were:

Petroleum consumed during one hour	1.378 gallons
Mean speed of engine	201rpm
Mean brake reading	4.26hp
Mean pressure, power cylinder	31psi
Mean pressure, air pump	27.6psi
Piston speed, motor	201 ft per minute
Piston speed, pump	100.5 ft per minute
Power indicated in motor	9.49hp
Power indicated in pump	4.10hp
Available indicated power	5.39hp

Therefore the mechanical efficiency of the engine is 79% and the consumption of fuel is 0.255 gallons per ihp and 0.323 gallons per bhp. The indicated thermal efficiency was only 6%. Fig. 4.16 shows typical indicator diagrams taken from the engine. Clerk thought the principle of the engine so good that he anticipated better results. The maximum

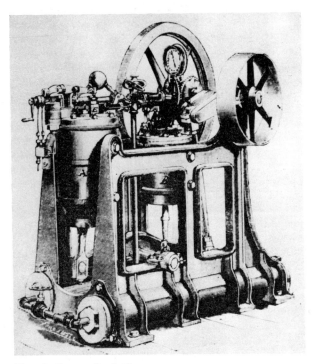

Plate 8 Brayton Ready Motor

pressure in the motor cylinder is 48psi, which remains steady till the inlet valve shuts at 40% of the stroke; the pressure then falls slowly as the gases expand, the exhaust valve opening at about 10psi above atmosphere. The maximum pressure in the air pump is 65psi, the reservoir being 60psi. The average pressure upon the power piston is 30.2psi and upon the air pump 27.6psi, which leaves only an effective pressure of 16.4psi to work the engine.

Dugald Clerk felt that if there were no losses of heat to the cylinder, or losses by throttling during the inlet and transfer of the air from the pump to the motor, or loss of heat from the reservoir to the atmosphere, then the efficiency of this type of engine would be 30%. However, in practice losses reduced this to 6%. The cycle, he felt, was a good one and under other circumstances was capable of better things, but was unsuitable in this form for a cold cylinder engine. Cooling and undue resistance were the main causes of the great deficit.

Several companies were involved in the construction and/or sale of Brayton oil engines, and they were the:

New New York and New Jersey Ready Motor Co. (1875)
The Pennsylvania Ready Motor Co. (1876)
The Brayton Ready Motor Co. Boston (1882)
Otto Neggiges, Berlin, was a licensee for a short time as was Thomson, Stern & Co., Glasgow, who employed Dugald Clerk.

The way ahead for the furnace gas engine was not in the slow speed reciprocating engine but in high speed gas turbines. Possibly the first detailed proposal for what would be now recognised as a gas turbine was put forward in 1853 by a Frenchman, M. Tournaire, in a paper presented to the Academie des Science from which the following is an extract:

APPLIED MECHANICS:- Notes upon multiple and successive reaction turbine devices for the utilization of the motive power developed by elastic fluids; by M. Tournaire, Ingenier des Mines. Commission: MM. Poncelet, Lame, Morin, Combes, Seguier.

Numerous attempts have been made to cause the vapour of water or other gaseous substances to act by reaction upon the blades or other hydraulic wheels; but down to the present time these inventions have not been crowned with practical success. The economical application of the principle of reaction to machines operated by elastic fluids would nevertheless be of a very high degree of interest, since the moving portions would thereby be reduced to very small dimensions, and motion would be lightened and simplified. In a word, such machines would enable the same advantages to be realized as are found with hydraulic turbines compared with water wheels of large diameter.

Elastic fluids acquire enormous velocities, even under the influence of comparatively low pressures. In order to utilize these pressures advantageously upon simple wheels analogous to hydraulic turbines, it would be necessary to permit rotary motion of extraordinary rapidity, and to use extremely minute orifices, even for a large expenditure of fluid. These difficulties may be avoided by causing the steam or gas to lose its pressure, either by successive fractions, making it react several times upon the blades of conveniently arranged turbines.

We must attribute the origin of the researches which we have made upon this subject to the communications which M. Burdin, Ingenieur des Mines, and Membre Correspondant de l'Institute, has had the courtesy to make to us, and which go back to the close of 1847. M. Burdin, who was then engaged upon a machine operated by hot air, desired to discharge the compressed and heated fluid upon a series of turbines fixed upon the same axis. Each one of these wheels was placed in a closed chamber, the air to be delivered through injector nozzles and discharged at a very low velocity. The author proposed to compress the cold air by means of a series of blowers arranged in a similar manner. This idea of employing a number of successive turbines in order to utilize the tension of the fluid a number of times seemed to us a simple and fertile one; we perceived in it the means of applying the principle of reaction to steam and air engines.

Since the differences in pressure, as used in steam engines, are considerable, it became evident that a large number of turbines would be required to give a sufficient reduction in the velocity of the fluid jet. The lightness and small dimensions of the moving parts permits of very high rotative speeds compared with those of ordinary engines.

Notwithstanding the multiplicity of parts, it is essential that the apparatus should be simple in its action, susceptible of a high degree of precision, and that adjustments and repairs should readily be made. We believe that we have fulfilled these essential conditions by means of the following arrangement:

A machine is composed of several independent motor axes, connected by means of pinions to a single wheel for the transmission of the motion. Each of these axes carries several turbines; these receive and discharge the fluid at the same distance from the axis.

Between two turbines is placed a fixed ring of guide blades. The guides receive the discharge from one reaction wheel and give it direction and velocity suitable to act upon the following wheel. Each of these systems of fixed and moving organs is to be enclosed in a cylindrical case. The guide blades will form portions of rings or annular pieces placed in the fixed cylinder, and these should be fitted very exactly the one to the other. The turbines should also have the form of rings, and should be fitted to a sleeve attached to the shaft. The first set of guides, which act simply as injector nozzles, may be made in one solid piece, carrying the journal of the shaft. Nothing could be easier than to erect or dismount such an apparatus. In order to transmit the motion it is necessary that the shaft should pass through the cylindrical case through an opening fitted with a tight packing; such a single stuffing box will answer for each series of reaction wheels.

After having acted upon the turbines on the first shaft, and thus parted with more or less of its elasticity, the fluid is caused to act upon the turbines of the second series, and so on. For this purpose large openings connect the end of each case with the beginning of the one which follows.

These cases and passages may form portions of the same casting. Since the steam or gas expands in proportion to its passage through the blades of the turbines it should be offered passage of continually increasing size, and the last portions of the apparatus will have much greater dimensions than the first . . .

. . . If hot air be substituted for steam, as we may hope from the beautiful and fertile experiments of Ericsson, our turbines will replace, very happily the enormous cylinders and pistons used by the Swedish engineer to receive the action of compressed air. It remains to be seen if similar rotative apparatus may not be usefully employed for the compression of cold air. In case of success a complete mechanical revolution will be effected not only with regard to the quantity of combustible consumed but also in the matter, not less important, of the masses and volumes which enter into machine construction.

Tournaire clearly foresaw the advantages of the gas turbine, that is: high fuel economy, high speed and reduction in size and weight, and foresaw the application of multistage turbines for both compression and delivery.

M. P. Boulton patented improvements in nozzles for gas turbines in 1864 (UK patent 1636) and investigated the problems of combustion at constant volume.

John Bourn took out patents in 1869 and 1870 for the combustion of coal dust to produce gases for use in a turbine. James Anderson took out patents for the combustion of air and gases in a turbine.

None of these plans seem to have been put into operation. In 1872 Dr F. Stolze, of Charlottenburg, near Berlin, applied for a patent for a 'Fire Turbine'. The experimental machine, built by Stolze, had a multi-turbine compressor and a multi-turbine power turbine, and was found to be of very low efficiency.

Although C. A. Parsons is now well known for his steam turbines, his patent of 1884 (UK patent 6735) makes references to gas turbines.

In 1893 De Laval proposed to deliver compressed air into a combustion chamber into which was sprayed liquid fuel, and the resultant products of combustion were to be directed on to a wheel, which is now known by his name.

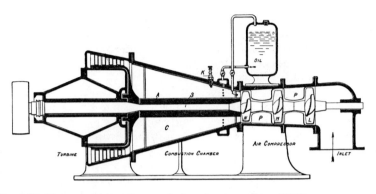

Fig. 4.17 Theoretical layout for a gradual combustion turbine (1912).

In a patent taken out by Ferranti in 1895 (UK patent 2565) the hot piston of a furnace gas engine was replaced by a De Laval type turbine. In a design by L. B. Atkinson in 1895 (UK patent 11955) the layout of the engine is similar to Brayton's engine with the motor piston replaced with a turbine. The combination of reciprocating air pump and rotary turbine would not have been a practical one.

Rankin Kennedy illustrated in 1912 a theoretical layout for a gradual combustion turbine (fig. 4.17).

Kennedy stated that:

> None are at present in the market but some promising designs exist and the principles of their construction can be laid down without the essential details for the practical success; these will come sooner or later, probably later, for the difficulties although not at all great their solution will cost much money, and the time required will be inversely as the money is expended . . . It is at present not the case that we do not know how to begin to make a combustion turbine for oil or gas; the difficulty is the great amount of time and expense required to bring the details to perfection, – an operation which can be effected only by actual experiments on a considerable scale of magnitude (20).

The development of the modern gas turbine dates from about 1930.

The Stirling brothers and the regenerative air engine

5

Although, as previously discussed, various ideas were put forward for increasing the efficiency of air engines by recovering some of the waste heat, the first practical idea was not put forward until 1816 when a patent was granted to the Rev Robert Stirling (1). Robert Stirling was born in 1790 in Cloag, Methvin, Perthshire. He was educated at St Andrews University and was ordained on 19th September 1816 at Kilmarnock, Ayrshire, in the Church of Scotland. In 1840 he was transferred to Galston, Ayrshire, where he stayed until his death. On May 30th 1842 he was, with nine others, suspended by the general assembly of the Church of Scotland from his judicial functions in the presbytery and the other higher courts for holding communion with deposed ministers of Strathbogie, but was reinstated on 1st March 1843; this was during disputes over the question of 'patronage'. He married Jane, eldest daughter of William Rankine, wine merchant, Galston, on 10th July 1819, and died on 6th June 1878 at Galston after two years of failing health.

In 1840 Robert Stirling received a degree of D.D. from the University of St Andrews, in recognition of his scholarly and scientific attainments. With slender means and living in isolation from engineering facilities, Stirling was compelled to carry out all his experiments himself. With his parish duties fully occupying his day, to get time for his experiments he rose early and worked late, particularly in the long summer evenings. His workshop was fitted with a heavy foot lathe, the bed of which was made of wood faced with iron plates, and most of his simple tools were of his own handiwork. Apart from building small experimental engines he constructed others of up to 2hp, making all the parts except the casting himself. He built an air engine to drive his lathe, boring the cylinder and heater on the lathe. Stirling did not give up his efforts to solve the problems of the air engine until he was nearly seventy, when he then turned his attention to astronomy, constructing many optical instruments. Of his sons, two of them, Patrick and James, became well known as locomotive engineers (2).

In his patent of 1816 Stirling made the claim that:

All my improvements for diminishing the consumption of fuel, consist of the differing forms or modification of a new method, contrivance, or mechanical arrangements for heating and cooling liquids, airs or gases, and other bodies, by the use of which contrivance heat is abstracted from one portion of such liquids, airs, and other bodies, and communicated to another portion with very little loss, so that in all cases where a constant succession of heated liquids or other bodies is required, the quantity of fuel necessary to maintain or supply it is by this contrivance greatly diminished.

He proposed several ways of reclaiming heat:

(a) A pipe is made either very narrow or with the bore very rough or with projections of metal or other materials, the hot liquid is first passed through it so giving up its heat, to the pipe with a temperature gradient along its length, the cold liquid to be heated is then passed through the pipe in the reverse direction.

(b) The heated fluid transmits its heat directly to the cold fluid, the two fluids flowing in opposite direction in pipes separated by a thin metal membrane.

Whilst (a) and (b) could be applied to heating and cooling fluids, (c) is a way to increase the temperature of a furnace. The furnace is fitted with two flues and air from a blowing engine is supplied to the fire through one flue whilst the hot waste gases pass out through the other, heating the flue walls in so leaving. If the process is then reversed the air on its way to the fire will be preheated by the flue walls, giving a fire of greater intensity than it would otherwise be. It is believed that the first application of the regenerative principle to iron smelting, by Robert Baired in 1825, was due to the suggestion of Robert Stirling, who apparently had originally included 'iron smelting furnace', in the original draft of his specification but had struck out the words and gave only one example, selecting a glass furnace for the purpose. Stirling's patent was cited at the famous hot blast trial of Neilson V. Baired & Co.,

Plate 9 Robert Stirling

in 1843, in proof of the absence of novelty in Neilson's invention, and this omission probably saved Neilson's patent. The term 'Regenerator' was coined later by Ericsson: Stirling preferred to call his invention an 'Economiser'. It is interesting to note that nearly all the applications of the regenerative principle in heating and cooling were foreseen by Stirling and indicated by him in his patent.

In applying his invention to an air engine Stirling built an engine that realised in a practical form the proposals that Thomas Mead had put forward in the patent of 1794. Like Mead, Stirling used a cylinder hot at one end and cold at the other, to shift the gases from one end to the other, but he used a hollow air tight cylinder, which he called a plunger, which was a loose fit in the cylinder, a better arrangement than Mead's proposed 'transferrer' that was a sliding fit and so would be a source of frictional losses. Stirling's first design placed the power piston in a separate cylinder to the plunger (fig. 5.1), but in his 1816 patent

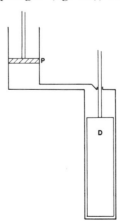

Fig. 5.1 Stirling, air engine

95

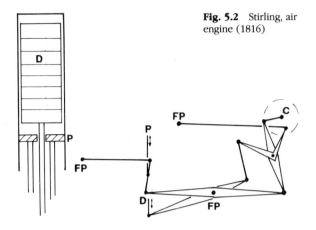

Fig. 5.2 Stirling, air engine (1816)

(fig. 5.2), the piston moved in the same cylinder as the plunger, as in Mead's layout, which he thought to be the best layout. The cylinder is formed of three parts, the lower of cast iron bored to take the power piston and the upper segments of sheet iron about ⅒in thick. The upper end is heated by a fire whilst the lower part is kept cold by water or a stream of air. Stirling took great care in designing his plunger, or displacer as it has now come to be called. To prevent the radiation of heat from the hot end to the cold end, so ensuring a good temperature gradient along its length, he divided it up into compartments separated by sheets of polished brass. To keep it from rubbing the sides of the cylinders the plunger was to be fitted with small wheels. Stirling used an inverted cylinder 'to prevent the oil used to render the piston air tight from getting to the hot parts and wasting the heat'. The gap between the wall of the cylinder and the plunger was about ⅕₀th of the whole diameter of the cylinder and was partly filled with turns of fine wire wound round the plunger and spaced from it and one another by wires laid along at right angles; this formed the regenerator.

The layout of the engine is really an inverted beam engine, with the piston connected by a straight line link motion to one end of a double beam which in turn drove the flywheel. To give motion to the plunger, a rod connected to the plunger passed through the centre of the piston onto a slider fitted to the piston rods, to render its motion steady and parallel. The slider was connected to a beam moving between the two power beams, the other end connected to a fixed point. By this means the plunger and piston move out of phase with each other. As the piston moves downwards under the pressure of the heated air, the crank rises

96

and the bent lever moves so as to raise the plunger. The air is then moved from the hot end to the cold, passing over the regenerator and so becoming cooled. The piston having been taken by the flywheel over dead centre is then pulled back up to its original position, and in doing so the crank moves down, causing the bent lever to move the plunger downwards, displacing the air back over the regenerator, where it takes back the heat lost into the hot end, so repeating the cycle. Assuming a temperature difference between the hot and cold part of 480°F, Stirling made the stroke of the plunger equal to that of the piston, the difference less the stroke of the plunger being such that it just touched the bottom of the cyliinder at the bottom of its stroke and the upper end of the cylinder on the other. The speed of the engine was governed by a valve, placed immediately above the highest ascent of the piston, that allowed a portion of the air to escape outwards or inwards.

In one of his early experiments Stirling had tried wire gauze in the space between the plunger and cylinder walls. An engine built in 1818 was constructed along the lines of his patent and was used to pump water from a quarry in Ayrshire, which work it performed well until, through the engine man's carelessness, the air vessel was overheated and, being made of boiler plate in a flat conical form, was crushed down by the air and so rendered useless. This engine did not work to the power expected, and Stirling deduced at the time that to build an engine with a larger power output the air vessel would need to be of enormous size, so the project was for a time abandoned. In 1824 Robert's brother James suggested that the problem might be surmounted and the dimensions of the engine greatly reduced by working with compressed air (3).

James Stirling (1809-76), like his elder brother, had first studied for the church but then directed his attention to mechanical engineering. He served an apprenticeship with the firm of Claud Girdwood & Co. of Glasgow and was subsequently engaged for some years as Engineer at their Deanston Works. He afterwards became Engineer and later Manager of the Dundee Foundry. Although the two brothers took out further patents in their joint names, the credit for improving Robert's original idea should go to the brother James. As an obituary to his brother, Robert Stirling wrote on 19th January 1876:

> It cannot be unreasonable, nay it is a duty in taking notice of the death of James Stirling, to make a remark which may stimulate the spirit of invention, or even contribute to realise its ambitious hopes. It is in fact, then, that he almost succeeded in establishing a new mechanical power, which promised to relieve the labours of that

gigantic and universal drudge the steam engine. He constructed at the Dundee Foundry an air engine which for three years performed all the work of that establishment, and failed at last from imperfections in the material of which it was constructed. These imperfections have in a great measure been removed by time, and especially by the genius of the distinguished Bessemer. If Bessemer iron or steel had been known thirty five or forty years ago, there is scarce a doubt that the air engine would have been a great success. But as the nature of cast iron forty years since required the hot part of the engine to be made three times thicker than it would now be, and consequently at least six times less fit for transmitting the heat, the outside of it required to be kept at a much higher temperature than would have been necessary with Bessemer iron. The hot part also was made convex, and required to be protected by a screen of bricks, the destruction of which by neglect implied the destruction of the engine; on the contrary, if the vessel had been concave and allowed to get a sight of the fire, as would now be easily accomplished, its operation would have been much more efficient, and the vessel, being equally heated, would not have been liable to crack.

The engine such as it was, worked to the extent of 40hp, according to the standard of Watt and Boulton; and this was ascertained not by theoretical calculations, but by proper application of the Trutsen strap and movable weights frequently used. Upon the whole, this experiment was conducted with such care and skill, and such jealousy of being deceived, that the result as to the power, &c., may be considered as fully established. It remains for some skilled and ambitious mechanist in the future age to repeat it under more favourable circumstances and with complete success (6).

The use of compressed air necessitated a closed cylinder or double acting with two air vessels. Having experimented with a working model constructed on this principle a patent was taken out in 1827 (UK patent 5456) jointly by Robert and James. The engine was to be fitted with an air pump, the stroke and diameter of which was half that of the power piston. The plunger or displacer had a stroke one-fourth that of the power piston but a diameter three times greater. The plunger and piston moved 90 deg out of phase, which meant that the plunger was at mid travel when the piston reversed its motion. The 1827 patent covered the construction of the plunger and air vessels, as having decided on an orthodox beam engine layout, James Stirling directed his efforts in seeking improvements in this quarter.

The air vessel was a cylindrical iron casting with a spherical bottom as

Fig. 5.3 Stirling, air vessel (1827)

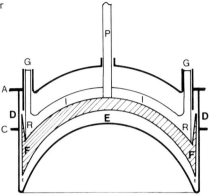

shown in fig. 5.3, with the section between the two flanges A and C turned internally to a smooth finish. Into this vessel is fitted the plunger, made up of the following parts: R a horizontal ring of cast iron supported by four irons I placed at equal distance round its circumference and joined at the centre to the push rod P of malleable iron. Each of the arms is fitted with a guide rod G which work in brasses, fixed in the cover of the air vessel, so as keep the plunger steady in its perpendicular motion. The ring, arms and guide rods are all cast in one piece and serve to support the plunger. To form the plunger a conical iron ring of sheet iron, DF, $\frac{1}{10}$in thick, is riveted to the ring at F, and at D to a cylindrical ring DE of sheet iron $\frac{1}{12}$in thick. A spherical plate EEE composed of plates of sheet iron, $\frac{1}{8}$in thick, riveted together and hammered so as to conform exactly to the contours of the air vessel bottom, is then joined by rivets at E. A similar spherical plate, FFF, $\frac{1}{16}$in thick, is riveted to the ring at F, so as to form a sheet iron box, where the distance between the two spherical plates is $3\frac{1}{2}$ to 4in, both being pierced by holes $\frac{1}{4}$in in diameter and not more than 1in apart. To ensure that the air passes through the box, a thin plate is fitted at D, split into thin strips. It extends round the whole circumference and the strips are bent outwards so as to lightly touch the turned part of the air vessel. To form the regenerator the box is filled with a layer of thin sheet iron plates pierced with holes and hammered into spherical form and kept at a distance of two or three times their own thickness from each other by small indentations. The fire is placed beneath the air vessel and the upper part kept cool by a stream of air or water. As the plunger is moved up and down air will be displaced from hot to cold end and vice-versa, being passed through the iron sheets, giving up and taking heat as it does so.

99

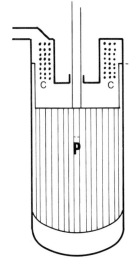

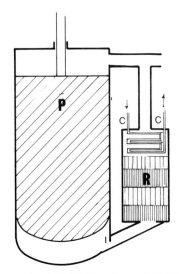

Fig. 5.4 Stirling, air vessel (1840) **Fig. 5.5** Stirling, air vessel (1840)

The engine, being double acting, was fitted with two displacer vessels, and an air pump was fitted to supply compressed air to an air tank, so that a supply of compressed air was always available for starting up or running the engine. Simple non-return was fitted to the supply line, with self acting valves fitted to the air pump. As an alternative to compressed air nitrogen and carbonic acid gas were also considered.

In 1828 an experimental engine was built at the works of Girdwood & Son. With a 26in diameter piston of 3ft stroke the engine gave about 20hp. It was found that the temperature of the cold end tended to rise so reducing the temperature differential with a corresponding fall off in power. In earlier experiments, because of the low power outputs air cooling had been sufficient, but with higher power output, the input of heat into the engine also went up, so the removal of waste heat became more important. James Stirling's solution was to place in the cold end coils of copper tubing through which water was passed. He built a small experimental engine of 2hp with a cylinder of 3⅝in and 12in stroke, and after trials lasting several months to test the efficiency of the cooling apparatus it was patented in 1840 (UK patent 8652).

Stirling's patent of 1840 was mainly concerned with detailing improvements made to the air vessels. In fig. 5.4 the cast iron air vessel is turned smooth internally, the cover is bolted to the upper flange and the joint made airtight by lead strip. The plunger P consists of an outer

100

shell of cast iron turned to give a sliding fit in the air vessel. The bottom of the plunger was to be perforated with air ways, the total area to be $\frac{1}{12}$th of the surface of the bottom of the plunger, and the interior was to be filled with strips of plain and fluted glass or closely packed glass rods, to act as a regenerator. The upper section of the air vessel was to be fitted with a cooler C consisting of a number of concentric plates or rings, through which water could be pumped.

In an alternative design the cooler and regenerator were placed outside the air vessel (fig. 5.5). The air vessel was to be formed of two parts, the upper turned smooth internally; the lower part forms the hot end and communicates with a cylindrical vessel, called a plate box, by means of three or more pipes. These, at their entrance into the air vessel, were to have a mouth that widened downwards and laterally covered with a fan-shaped plate I intended to spread the air with great velocity over the whole of the spheroidal bottom. The plunger P was turned to give a reasonable fit in the air vessel and occupies about $\frac{5}{8}$ of the air vessel. In order to lessen the radiation of heat from one end of the plunger to the other a quantity of pounded bricks was used to fill the lower part, the remainder being divided into 12 to 16 compartments by iron plates. A plate of cast iron was also to be fitted to the bottom of the plunger. To form a regenerator the plate box was to be $\frac{2}{5}$ filled with thin iron sheets, about $\frac{1}{40}$in thick and kept $\frac{1}{50}$in apart by dimples or ridges in the sheets. The sheets were to be stacked into four or more sections to reduce heat conduction.

The remainder of the box was to be filled with a cooler consisting of copper tubes $6\frac{3}{4}$in long and about $\frac{1}{8}$in internal diameter, the pipes to be arranged in 27 horizontal rows with each alternate row having one pipe less, so that each row would be placed at the intercesses of the previous row, ensuring that the air would flow around the pipes rather than passing over them. The pipes were separated by about $\frac{1}{20}$in.

The patent gives the swept volume of the power cylinder as about $\frac{7}{10}$ of the air vessel, the movement of the plunger being 75 deg in advance of the piston. The air supply pump was to be equal in stroke to the power piston but $\frac{5}{12}$ of its diameter, and was to be kept cool by a water jacket. It would seem that the first experiments in air vessel design were along the lines of the layout first described, the placing of the cooling outside the air vessel being a development probably when it was found that more efficient cooling takes place when the air is blown over the tubes.

In building his air engines, Robert Stirling chose to use modified steam engines, using the cylinder and flywheel as in a beam engine, the plunger being driven by cranks or eccentric and the air pump replacing the condenser pump of the steam engine. This layout has disdvantages over the 1816 engine in that the use of separate air vessels meant additional pipework, so increasing the air inside the engine that was not heated or cooled but merely shifted through the pipe work. This has come to be called the dead space and by lowering the compression ratio it reduces the power of the engine. This must have become apparent to the Stirlings as it is stated in their patent 'As every portion of the space within the air vessel, cylinder, plate box and passages takes in a quantity of air when the pressure is increased, and gives out a quantity when the pressure is diminished, so as to impare the impulse given to the piston, we carefully guard against all unnecessary space in the interior of the engine, and in particular we make the passages as narrow as is consistent with the easy motion of the air.' James Stirling further tried to reduce the dead space by expanding the air in the hot end of the air vessel directly on to the piston; he protected the piston from the higher temperature by fitting a crown filled with non-conducting materials (in much the same way as tried by Cayley) but he had little success (4).

When working his engines at atmospheric pressure Stirling found that the power output barely overcame frictional losses, but the more the pressure was raised the better the engine worked. A small engine was worked at a pressure of 360psi, but the problem of working with what was at that time considered a high pressure was making a good airtight casting and rendering joints sufficiently airtight; it was found difficult to make airtight joints above 150psi.

The main weakness in the air vessels was the bottoms, which for want of a better material were made out of cast iron and since they were kept at a red heat soon burnt out, so that they had to be increased in thickness at the base to some 4in to give a longer operating life. This led to a reduction in the efficiency of heat transfer. A variety of air vessel shapes was tried, among them a bottle shape which gave good results, but a hemispherical shape proved best. The possibility of the bottom falling out presented no danger of explosion: Patrick Stirling, who was present on two occasions when the air vessels on the Dundee engine failed, stated that the only inconvenience felt was getting a little black smoke thrown in his face. The air escaped in about two seconds and occurred in air vessels with bottle shaped bottoms, the vessels being made of cast iron with a little copper in it, which it was claimed greatly increased the strength (5).

Following Robert Stirling's early experiments with wire gauze, various forms of regenerator were tried. In the 1827 patent the idea was to separate all plates from each other so as to give an even temperature gradient across the stack. James then tried dividing up the plates into five portions, but he found that when the engine was running no advantage was observed, and after numerous experiments he reverted to a continuous regenerator. When the engine was at rest the conducting power of the regenerator had the tendency to equalise the temperature throughout the engine, but a few minutes after it had been set in motion, the temperature along the regenerator was such that it diminished from hot to cold end as heat was given up to, and taken in from, the passing air. It was found that the narrower the air passage the more efficient the regenerator became.

In 1842 James Stirling converted the steam engine that drove the machinery at the Dundee Foundry. He removed the boiler, air pump and condenser but made use of as many parts of the steam engine as was possible. An earlier engine had been built with a cylinder of 12in diameter with a stroke of 2ft, which when running at 40rpm gave 21hp with a fuel consumption of 50lb of coal per hour. This engine drove all the machinery at the Dundee works for some eight to ten months, but this was found too small for the requirements of the works so the bigger engine was built. The new cylinder had a diameter of 16in and a 4ft stroke, but the use of the beam engine parts limited the speed to 28rpm and so restricted the power that could be obtained.

On test the engine gave, by means of a friction brake on a third mover, nearly 1,500,000 lb ft (45.5hp). It was found difficult to maintain the load steady for any length of time as the strap became heated, but the engine was worked for a whole day with a measured burden of 1,250,000 lb ft (37.8hp) as well as driving three extensive lines of shafting of 370ft in length. The engine did this for a consumption of 1000lb of Scotch chew coals, including the quantity required for raising heat in the morning and maintaining it during the two hours for meals when the works usually stopped. These coals were claimed to be of inferior quality and to be at least one fourth less capable of producing heat than ordinary English coals. By taking this into account and deducting 150lb that was found necessary for raising heat, Stirling gave a consumption of 600lb in 12 hours. The power requirement for the foundry was some 21hp.

The engine was started up in March 1843, and gave an immediate saving in fuel. James Stirling claimed that where the steam engine used 26cwt, the air engine needed only 6cwt, but the steam engine that it had replaced had not been of the best construction and had no boiler cladding. James Stirling saw these results, though not as favourable as he had hoped, as an indication of what the air engine was capable of. Little had been done in improving the furnace as all effort had been directed to heating the air vessels without regard to economy of fuel. Coal was supplied to the fire by a feeding apparatus, with regulating doors to the ash pit, so as to reduce the unnecessary introduction of cold air which would have been the case had hand stoking been used. The fire grate was 24in by 22in, and it was found that the damper in the furnace flue was nearly always kept closed.

When the engine was running at 21hp, 4 cu ft of water per minute were passed through the cooler tubes and thence into a cistern to cool, to be used again. This reduced air temperature by some 150 to 160°F, the water being raised by 16 to 18°F. Indicator diagrams were taken and were oval in shape, but they were not considered reliable because of excessive friction in the indicator. No temperature measurements were taken of the hot end, but as the air vessels were kept at a red heat this was assumed to be 650°F. The working pressure varied during each stroke from between 160 to 240psi, the lower pressure being maintained by the air feed pump (7).

The air vessels (fig. 5.6), were of 4ft internal diameter with a height of about 8ft (6). A solid plunger P was used and the improved cooler C placed in the top of the air vessel. The regenerator R was formed from about 3350 thin metal plates 38in long by 1.75in broad and 0.02in thick. These plates were placed ⅟₃₂in apart around the air vessel walls as if radiating out from the centre, giving some 3200 sq ft of surface area, the amount of air contained in the air vessels being about 9 cu ft. The fire did not act on the vessels directly, as it was placed in a central space from which the hot gases passed into chambers containing the air vessels, formed of firebrick. The packing of the plunger rods was as detailed in the 1840 patent. A copper tube filled with a solution of pitch and oil was fixed to the top of the plunger and into this dipped a pipe attached to the stuffing box, the idea being to prevent air getting to the leather collar that encircled the plunger rod, so that, as Patrick Stirling put it: 'by no amount of pressure could any air get through'. James Stirling, however, was not so optimistic, saying that since the plunger rods were generally at 150°F there was no difficulty in keeping the stuffing box almost perfectly airtight.

The piston was fitted with two cast iron rings made self springing, of the type then in common use in steam engines. The piston rod was fitted with a leather exactly like the plunger of a Bramer press, but it seems that these leather seals would only last about two or three months. It was claimed that a gill of oil would be sufficient to lubricate the piston and plunger rods for two days. To enable the power output

104

to be easily varied the stroke of the plungers could be shortened or lengthened, by means of a hand wheel driving a screw via bevel gears, so that the effective length of the lever driving the plunger could be changed; This was made self-acting by means of a Watt governor.

An inspection made after the engine had been in service for two and a half years revealed no perceptible wear and the cylinder had attained a high polish. The regenerator was not corroded, nor was there any dust or dirt in the air vessels.

The first sign of trouble came in December 1845 when an air vessel burnt out. This was replaced, but the engine only ran until May 1846 when the second bottom burnt out. The engine was again repaired but a third bottom burnt out in January 1847. James Stirling had left the foundry in 1846 and the new owners, discouraged by the results, removed the air engine and reconverted to a steam engine. Mr David Mundie, one of the new lessees of the foundry, found the motion of the air engine was not perfectly smooth and uniform, which was the only mechanical objection, but the only reason for the reconversion was that the air vessels could not be built to withstand the heat to which they were exposed.

The workings of the hot air engine were not at that time fully understood and were the cause of much discussion. The engines were made without the aid of modern thermodynamics and metallurgy and were a triumph for the practical engineer. That Stirling ultimately failed was

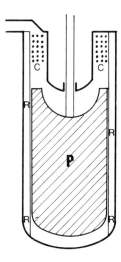

Fig. 5.6 Stirling, air vessel (1842)

not due to lack of design, though using a steam engine layout was a drawback, but more through the need for high temperature metals and engineering techniques not then available, as witnessed by the difficulty of constructing airtight joints at what was then considered high pressures and the limitation placed on upper temperature by the use of cast iron, which severely limited the efficiency of the engine.

Stirling's greatest achievement was in perfecting the regenerator, the workings of which were little understood and the effectiveness hotly debated. Where others doubted the usefulness Robert Stirling was in no doubt, as when he gave the following description of the working of his economiser:

> To demonstrate the efficiency of the 'regenerator' or as it might be more properly called the 'economiser' we only have to assume as an axiom what is universally known and believed; that two bodies of unequal temperatures will speedily be equalised. We also require as in other physical demonstration, to lay out of consideration all circumstances that are not essential such as the gradual dissipation of caloric by radiation etc. It will also simplify the demonstration if we confine our attention to the change produced upon the temperature of the air and suppose that of the parts of the apparatus to remain invariable. This approaches very near to the truth, even in practice, since the capacity for the caloric in the apparatus must be vastly greater than that of the mass of air to be heated and cooled.

> Now let A be a minute portion, or particle of air, at a temperature of 50°, and let B C D E F G H I J K be points or portions of the economiser having the temperatures respectively attached to them, let A be brought into contact with B and it will immediately acquire the temperature of 60°, let it touch C and it will be raised to 70° and so on till at last by contact with K it acquires the temperature of 150°, having been heated in all 100° and having taken only 10° from each point or body in the series. The same thing will also hold good in all successive particles of air which comprise the whole mass to be heated.

A	
B	60°
C	70°
D	80°
E	90°
F	100°
G	110°
H	120°
I	130°
J	140°
K	150°
A	

Suppose further, that by any means the temperature (of A) has been raised to 160° – has attained its maximum and requires to be cooled. For this purpose let it be applied to K and it fall to 150°, then to J and it becomes 140° and so on till at last meeting with B, it has cooled to 60°. It has thus lost 100°, imparting only 10° to each of the points to which it was applied. If now by any means 10° be abstracted from it, it will reduce to its original temperature of 50°. In the process of being heated it has imbibed $10/11$ths of its maximum temperature from the bodies represented by B C D, etc and in the process of being cooled it has returned the very same quantity to these bodies, distributing its caloric equally and giving 10° to each member of the series.

Let this process be repeated and it is evident that at every successive heating and cooling the air requires only 10° to be added to the temperature acquired from the series of bodies B C D, to raise it to its supposed maximum of 160° and at every successive cooling it requires only 10° to be abstracted to bring it to the original temperature of 50°. And thus it appears that by applying air successive to a series of bodies regularly increasing in temperature and moving it alternately from one end of the series to the other, it may be *heated and cooled ten times*, with an expenditure of caloric which would have barely heated it once, if it been applied at *once* to the hottest body (i.e. beyond the series). It is evident also that if the series had been composed of twenty points, or bodies, having a difference of temperature of 5° the air might be *heated and cooled twenty times* at no greater expense of caloric. Nay it seems evident, that by multiplying the members of the series *indefinitely* air could be heated and expanded and made to work at *no appreciable expense*. But let no mathematician be alarmed with the idea of perpetual motion, or a creation of power. There are many enemies to contend with in the air engine besides friction which alone prevents perpetuity in some mechanical motions. We have no means, without consuming a part of our power, of applying the air so closely to the apparatus as to make it absolutely assume the temperature of the bodies to which it is applied.

There is therefore a loss in the very act of heating and cooling. The change of temperature that takes place in each place of the economising bodies, during the passage of the air, though small, yet prevents the *absolutely* uniform heating of the whole mass, and thus causes waste. But the greatest enemy of the economising principle is the continual passage of the caloric from the hot part to the cold parts of the engine, by radiation, conduction, etc., which require a continual supply of the caloric to maintain the proper temperature of each. This defect however is not peculiar to the air engine and by multiplying the steps by which the caloric must make its way in escaping, and by opposing various obstacles to its progress, we can detain it as to make it frequently perform the duty of expansion before it altogether escapes.

The Stirling brothers were not alone in building engines of the displacer type. In 1827 a patent (no. 5530) was granted to William Parkinson and Samuel Crosly for an engine design by Parkinson and designed to run on town gas. Samuel Crosly was a gas apparatus manufacturer and no doubt saw an extra line of business. It would seem that only a working model was made, and this ran at some 150rpm. The model was still in existence some twenty years later when it was demonstrated at a meeting of the Civil Engineers held on the 17th May, 1853. No claim was made for originality in the use of heated air but novelty was claimed for the use of the displacer (fig. 5.7) T is the transferrer, W the cooling water and G the gas heating ring.

To quote from the patent:

> The power of our improved engine is to be produced by heating and cooling air. The air is to be heated and cooled in air tight vessel, which we term a differential vessel, a portion of which is exposed to external heat and a portion to external cold. Within this vessel is contained another which we call a transferrer. The transferrer being moved from the hot to the cold parts of the differential vessel, and from the cold to the hot alternately, thereby transfers the air, and subjects it to the heat and the cold as it passes along the internal surfaces of the differential vessel, and thus by the expansion and contraction of the air produces force for giving motion to the machinery. We do not claim originality in producing power by expanding and contracting air, nor in the application of heat and cold for that purpose. Various forms of vessels have been employed for the purpose of heating and cooling air: but the peculiarity of our method consists in transferring the air to the hot and cold part of the

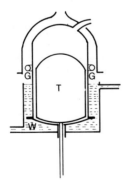

Fig. 5.7 Parkinson and Crosly, air vessel (1827).

differential vessel by means of a transferrer which is solid, and which may fill a great proportion of the differential vessel, but the transferrer maybe made hollow if made of sufficient strength to prevent its collapsing.

The engine did not have a regenerator but it did have water cooling and the effect of air density on the power of the engine was realised. It was stated in the patent that:

We have stated that the power of the engine will in some measure depend upon the density of the air in the differential vessel. If therefore it is desired to increase the power of the engine by increasing the density of the air, a common forcing pump, to be worked by the engine, and connected with the differential vessel, must be applied and as some leakage of air may be anticipated at the high pressures, the addition of the pump is necessary . . . this pump may be of the usual construction of forcing pumps, and must be provided with any of the well known means of adapting the length of its stroke to the loss of air by leakage.

Small engines built along the lines of Parkinson's engine were to provide a more useful alternative source of small power to the steam engine, and later the oil and gas engine, than did the larger steam engine conversions of James Stirling. The availability of town gas was to enable small hot air engines to be used for domestic and other non-industrial purposes. It was claimed in the patent that: 'the use of gas to our engine, and the application of the means we have described for obtaining a supply, enables us to furnish a compact power engine, not requiring the constant attendance of a fireman, and adapted to situations where sufficient space could not be appropriated for an engine requiring a boiler . . .'

Following the pioneering work of the Stirling brothers many patents for displacer type engines were granted, covering improvements in heat exchangers, regenerators, special displacer drives etc. in a wide variety of mechanical layouts. The practical form of engine that evolved from all these many patents was one of low efficiency, slow running and having at best a primitive form of regeneration but with the great practical advantages of being able to burn a wide variety of fuels, being simple to operate and maintain and having a long operating life.

Two basic forms evolved, large coal fired engines for pumping water and driving light machinery and small domestic motors burning gas or lamp oil, used in driving petrol/air gas plants, powering ventilating fans or pumping air into fish tanks.

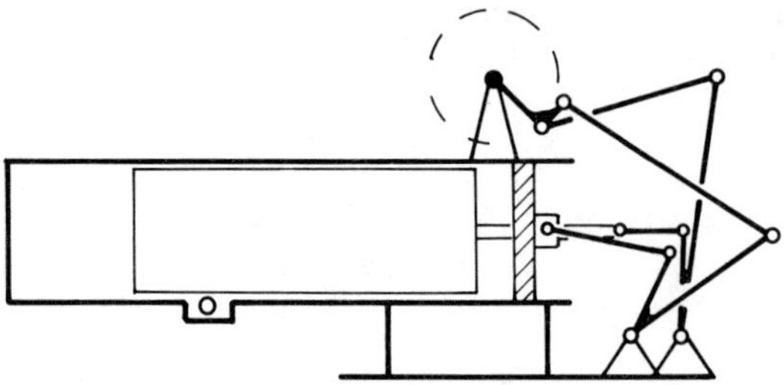

Fig. 5.8 Lemann, air engine (1868)

In a design developed by Joseph Francois Laubereau, of Paris, a cam was used to drive the displacer to give a rapid intermittent motion with a dwell at the end of each stroke. The power cylinder was separate from the displacer and was connected to the hot end of it, and cooling was by circulating water through a jacket around the top of the displacer cylinder.

The design was covered by several British and French patents, e.g.UK patents 213, 1859; 1809, 1864; 2364, 1874.

One of Laubereau's engines was tested by Professor Tresca, in Paris over a period of six days (7). He found that the engine needed to be heated for a period of one hour before it could be started.

The following data was given in his report:

Dia. working cylinder	500mm
Stroke	400mm
Speed	37rpm
Phase difference	90 deg
Useful power developed per/sec	0.8hp
Mechanical efficiency	0.4
Fuel consumption 4.5-5kg of coke per hour per hp	
Calculated overall efficiency	1.8%

A successful engine used in Britain and the Continent was one based on a design by W. Lemann of 1868 (fig. 5.8). Lemann used a long horizontal cylinder with concentric piston and displacer, a return to Stirling's original design of 1816. About one third of the cylinder was heated with the remaining length kept cool with a water jacket. With such a long displacer it was necessary to give support to it with rollers set just at the end of the cooling jacket. The motion of the displacer was set 65 deg in advance of the power piston, using a driving mechanism from an overset crank in a manner very similar to that used by Ericsson in his caloric engines. In a report by Eckerth (9) the following details are given:

110

Plate 10 Laubereau engine

Plate 11 Bailey horizontal engine

Fig. 5.9 Indicator diagram, Bailey engine

Dia. of working piston	349mm
Stroke	175mm
Dia. of displacer	342mm
Stroke	244mm
Length	1527mm
Phase difference	65 deg
Speed	100rpm
Indicated mean effective pressure	0.44kg/sq cm
Indicated power	118.3mkg
Brake power	76mkg
Mechanical efficiency	0.64
Calculated overall efficiency	4%

A mean average of the friction brake was given as 0.984bhp. The indicator diagram gave a rise of pressure of in excess of 10lb and also gave a slight vacuum, which Lemann utilised to maintain power lost by air leakage by using a snifter valve to draw in a fresh charge of air. Fig. 5.9 shows an indicator diagram taken from a Bailey engine.

RPM	106
Stroke	6⅞in
Diameter	14⅝in
IHP	2.37
BHP	1.31
Mech efficiency	55%

Delbar, reporting on tests undertaken on Lemann's engine, made the following comments (10):

As regards to the working piston it is sealed by leather packing, bent towards the inside. It acts as a valve opening towards the inside of the cylinder.

Any loss of air is replaced at each revolution by means of the packing itself, and, consequently, a decrease of the volume of the working air can never occur.

When the air in both spaces has almost the same pressure, then the pressure in one space is based on a high temperature, and in the other on a high density, thus rarefied hot air is in one space and compressed cold air in the other.

112

The working piston in Lemann's engine is consequently subject only to the effect of the compressed cooled air, whereas in Laubereau's it is exposed to the direct effect of the heated air.

Delbar listed what he thought to be twelve advantages of Lemann's engine:

1. It works without noise.

2. All the parts subject to friction work in cool conditions, and thus they can be greased from common oil, and are less liable to being worn out.

3. It does not spoil the air in the room, and there is no smell of oil.

4. It can be placed on upper floors, and a common flue is quite sufficient.

5. There is no danger of explosions, no licence of authorities is required, no higher premium is paid for fire insurance.

6. Managing is simple, no special help is necessary, any boy or worker can fire the engine.

7. Any fuel can be used.

8. In a short time, after 15 or 20 minutes of firing, it can be put to work.

9. The firing of the engine can also be used for cooking and heating the room.

10. Cooling water is contained in a single reservoir; it always remains pure and can be used as hot water for different purposes.

11. In as few as twenty minutes it can be disassembled and ssembled again, if anything goes wrong.

12. At a moderate price when compared to similar engines.

A number of different models, both vertical and horizontal, were developed from Lemann's basic design, the manufacture being taken up by the Berlin Anhaltische Maschinenbau Actien Gesellschaft for water pumping. (UK patent 1565, 1874).

In Britain the manufacture was taken up by W. H. Bailey of the Albion Works, Salford, who patented improvements covering the three types of engines they sold (UK patent 1357, 1881).

The three types sold by Bailey's were a 'Horizontal' engine for pumping and driving machinery, sold in six sizes ranging up to 5hp. The engine required a firebrick furnace to be built, but it was claimed that this could be erected in a day by any ordinary brick-setter to instructions sent with each engine; the firebox was designed to produce a slow combustion and to require little attention. An engine for pumping water came with an integral water pump, but for driving machinery additional driving gear was required. An engine fitted with a

Plate 12 Robinson engine

Plate 13 Essex engine

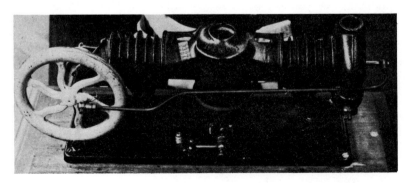

3in pump delivering 1000 gallons to a height of 85ft would be in size: 9ft 9in long overall by 3ft 8in wide and to the top of the flywheel 4ft 10in high and the approximate weight would be one ton. For their engine the makers claimed:

> The furnace will burn almost any fuel – coke, coal, peat, wood, sawdust, spent tan, riddled cinders, etc. and as it consumes its own smoke it needs no attention during the intervals of firing. Thus it will be seen that the attention required is so simple, and of a light nature, that any intelligent lad, workman, labourer, gardener or domestic servent may learn to work it in a few hours with the assistance of our printed instruction, and attend to it without material interference with their other occupation.

For lighter duties there was the 'Vertical' pumping engine for shallow wells, in three sizes ⅟16, ⅛ and ¼hp. Depending on the engine size and the diameter of the water pump delivery was from 150 to 1600 gallons per hour from 80 to 30ft. The engines were priced at £40, £50 and £60.

The third engine was called the 'Bee' and came in two sizes priced at £15 and £20 and it was claimed that it could be driven at a cost of one farthing per hour by gas jet with a bunsen burner.

An engine developed by O. Stenberg, of Helsingsfors, in 1877 (UK patent 3159) followed the general layout of Lemann's engine but used an intermittent drive to the displacer. The drive was a form of cam or modified scotch yoke consisting of a roller working in a slot shaped as a segment of a circle of large diameter, the idea being as in Laubereau's engine to give a dwell at the end of the displacer stroke.

Many small hot air engines for domestic use, sold in manpowers rather than horsepowers, were produced, and one successful British design was the Robinson engine.

In a patent granted to Arnold and Horace Robinson in 1881 (UK patent 5056) a vertical engine with concentric piston and displacer was described, with cooling by means of a water jacket surrounding the top of the cylinder. The displacer itself formed a moving regenerator, air passing through the body of the displacer as it moved. Robinson engines were one of the few designs where an attempt was made to fit a proper form of regenerator.

In patent granted in 1886 (no. 11,346) Horace Robinson departed from the vertical design for one with a vertical displacer and horizontal power cylinders, giving a squat but less efficient design. The displacer again formed a moving regenerator. An improved form of displacer drive was given in a patent of 1889 (no. 298) (fig. 5.10), also a form of speed control was described; a lightly loaded valve was used to throttle the air passage between the displacer and cylinder when the speed rose too high. Further improvements in the linkwork were made in a patent granted to H. Lewis in 1907 (no. 26,944). Robinson engines to the 1889 design were produced by several Manchester and London firms, including Pearce & Son, Norris & Henty and L. Gardener & Sons, Norris and Henty patenting improvements in the heating chamber in 1898 (no. 20,538).

These engines worked on a low pressure cycle and had no means of making up lost air and were therefore relatively large for the power given out.

Size	BHP approx.	Bore inches	Dimensions inches	Weight c:q:lbs	RPM
4	$\frac{1}{11}$	$5\frac{1}{2}$	34×26×40	4:3:12	150-210
5	$\frac{1}{4}$	$7\frac{1}{2}$	45×35×35	8:2:7	150-190
6	$\frac{5}{8}$	10	55×50×41	15:2:0	140-170

These engines found wide use in pumping water, driving petrol/air plants, coffee grinders, etc. The firm of W. T. Sugg, gas equipment makers, also used the Robinson for driving gas compressors, the compressor being driven direct from the power cylinder (UK patents 24,986, 1904 and 16,477, 1905) with the body of the engine having an extension to carry the compressor directly in line with the piston.

Another widely used domestic motor was the Heinrici engine designed by Louis Heinrici of Zwickau in Saxony. These engines were

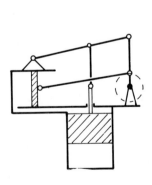

Fig. 5.10 Robinson, hot air engine (1886)

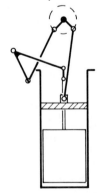

Fig. 5.11 Heinrici, air engine (c.1895)

well made and compact, the smaller power engines operating from gas or lamp oil and the larger could be coal fired. Two designs were produced, a small engine with separate power cylinder and displacer and a larger and more powerful engine with concentric piston and displacer (fig. 5.11).

The smaller engine, for very light work, had a 30mm dia. piston and was offered water-cooled at 1/200hp priced at £3.3.0d or, without cooling, at 1/500hp, price £2.15.0d.

The larger engines were all water-cooled and sold in eight sizes from 40mm piston (1/100hp) up to 190mm (2/5hp), priced from £4.5.0d to £48.

Heinrici took out many patents for improvements:

UK patent	no. 2629	1898
Patentschrift	no, 109983	1899
	no. 132447	1901
	no. 140172	1903
Patent	no. 22540	1899
	no. 38505	1906
Gebraudmunster	no. 264479	1904
	no. 288423	1905
	no. 289570	1906
	no. 354898	1908

In a design by Dirk Willen Van Rennes, of Utrecht, an oscillating power cylinder was used. The displacer cylinder was set vertical with the top water cooled and it was moved by a walking beam, the connection between power cylinder and displacer cylinder being made with a rubber tube (UK patents 1304, 1876 and 1750, 1879).

In a report by Slaby (*Dingler's Poly Journal*, 1879) the following details were given:

Dia. of power piston	261mm
Stroke	297mm
Dia. of displacer	500mm
Stroke	493mm
Length	965mm
Phase angle	95 deg

An engine was reported in 1878 to be working in an Amsterdam factory pumping 28.5 gallons of water per minute to a height of 18ft.

The method used by Van Rennes for pumping water has some similarity with a Pulsometer pump. The pump consisted of two chambers, one set above the other and linked by a pipe, with the lower

Plate 14 Van Rennes engine

chamber connected to the water to be raised by a suction pump. Each chamber was fitted with a non return valve. The lower chamber was also connected to the displacer cylinder of the engine and as the displacer was lifted the air pressure in the engine rose and so acted on the surface of the water in the lower chamber, driving it up into the upper chamber. When the displacer was lowered the pressure fell and water was drawn up the suction pipe into the lower chamber, thus producing a cycle giving a continual flow of water.

A small domestic motor with an oscillating piston was patented by Adam Koerber, London, in 1887 (UK patent 2844). In the *English Mechanic* for 1886 the inventor described a machine he had used for two years to drive a wire covering machine. The vertical displacer cylinder was water cooled and stood 13in high and 6.5in diameter, the

118

power cylinder was 2⅝in in diameter with a stroke of 4in, and a 16in flywheel was fitted.

Henry Essex of Buffalo, New York, patented in 1903 (US patent 723,660) a design that kept the air acting on the piston hot. In his design the flame from a gas burner was applied to the middle of the engine and not at the end as would be normal. In his patent Essex noted:

> In other hot air engines having the displacer piston operating in the same cylinder the furnace has been placed at the end of the cylinder, and the full effect of the expanding air could not be exerted on the working piston because the air has to pass the cool end of the displacer-piston and become cooled before it could get at the working piston, and consequently in such engines only about half as long a stroke as that of the displacer piston could be obtained for the working piston. My improvement of the placing of the furnace midway of the cylinder gets the expanding hot air directly and with full effect against the working piston, and consequently makes about as long a stroke for the working piston as for the displacer piston, thus doubling the efficiency.

In a small ventilating fan Essex took the design further by making the crown of the piston the hot end of the engine. The flame from a gas burner was played on to the piston as it moved up and down, the displacer being moved from the opposite end by means of a scotch yoke.

Many designs appeared for improvements in displacer cylinder design, most seeking to improve heat transfer, by the use of corrugated surfaces etc. A rotary displacer was proposed in 1888 by J. Trewhella (UK patent 9212).

There have in recent years been a number of designs published for non-rotative Stirling engines. However, the first designs appeared, for use in gas lamps, at the turn of the century.

Gas compressors for incandescent lamps

Some early designs for hot air driven gas or air compressors took the form of a conventional displacer engine heated by the waste heat of the gas burner and a typical layout is found in patent granted to the Newprocess Lighting Co of Cleveland, USA (UK patents 21,622, 1900 and 18,133, 1902). This uses a conventional rotating engine that was started by pulling round the flywheel by ratchet and chains.

The alternative was to use some form of non-rotating engine.

William Chipperfield – 1907

A patent was granted to Edward Cook and William Chipperfield, both from London, in 1907, (UK patent 20,521). Fig. 5.12 gives the general layout. D is the displacer, its weight being held in suspension by a spring S. F is a flexible diaphragm that forms the body of the gas pump. V is a cylindrical slide valve, connecting the interior of the engine with the atmosphere. The mode of operation is as follows:

1. At rest the engine is as shown.
2. If heat is applied the air pressure rises and will expand against the diaphragm, forcing it upwards and in turn pulling up the displacer, so moving air from cold to hot end causing further rise in pressure.
3. At a certain point the displacer strikes the valve V pushing it open and so releasing the pressure within the engine.
4. The displacer now falls.
5. At a certain point the displacer rod strikes the valve and closes it. The cycle can now be repeated.

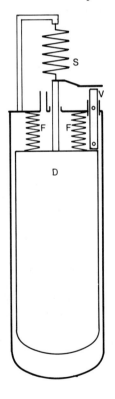

Fig. 5.12 Chipperfield, gas pump (1907)

The motion imparted to the flexible diaphragm causes it to act as a pump, drawing in gas or air and passing it to the lamp burner.

Further improvements were patented in 1909 (UK patent 8450) in the name of the Chipperfield Lamp Syndicate & E. M. Browning.

Stuart Merrick – 1912

In this design by Stuart Merrick of Hornsey, London (UK patent 15,665) the motor (fig. 5.13), consists of two diaphragms. D1 the power piston of the machine and D2 the piston of the gas or air pump. D1 and D2 are linked together by a bellcrank B and two links, L1 and L2 so that on the up stroke of D1 a downward or suction stroke is performed by D2. The relationship between the strokes of each is set by the relative lengths of the two arms on the bellcrank.

The power diaphragm and displacer DP are coupled through a system of links to a horizontal bar H. H rises and falls and is suspended from adjustable springs S. The relationship between length of stroke of the two is set by the position of the pivot P along the length of link L and is set such that the stroke of the displacer is greater than that of the diaphragm.

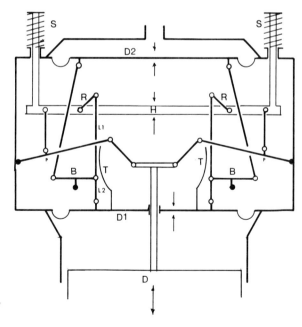

Fig. 5.13 Merrick, gas pump (1912)

The two links R are pressed upon by a spring T in such a way as to ensure that H will be depressed when D1 is raised; this will in turn cause DP to fall.

The displacer moves air in the normal manner from hot to cold end of the heater chamber. If DP falls air is shifted to the cold end and the pressure acting on D1 drops and will cause it to fall. Link R falls below the level of attachment with H which is then forced up, so raising DP, and the pressure again rises.

The displacer (being practically floating on the side springs) is easily operated by light springs attached to the overhead pumping diaphragm or other part moving therewith. This diaphragm movement upwards naturally synchronises with the downward or vacuum stroke of the power diaphragm, due to the downward travel of the displacer, it tends therefore to restore the displacer to its upper position, but having first arrested the downward movement and set the mass in motion in the reverse direction, it is late in point of time and only succeeds at or near the end of the power stroke. Whilst its energy is being expressed in the motion upward of the displacer the vacuum becomes spoiled and the pull of the springs falls off by the falling down of the upper diaphragm. The displacer having continued its travel under the initial impulse ultimately falls downward again once more restoring power to the operating springs and repeating the cycle.

The displacer chamber was heated from the waste heat rising from the gas mantle.

Free piston engines

In the true free piston engine there is no mechanical linkage coupling the piston and displacer together. The reciprocating interaction of piston and displacer is effected by utilizing the fluid forces of the enclosed gases. The free piston concept was developed in America by William Beal in the late 1950s, whilst he was Professor of Mechanical Engineering at the University of Ohio. Over the next decade he developed the concept to a practical stage, but unable to secure funds he went on to found the company Sunpower Inc. of Athens, Ohio, to develop and market the engine.

The Beal engine consists of three basic components, a heavy piston, a lightweight displacer and a cylinder sealed at both ends, as shown in fig. 5.14. A is the lightweight displacer, C the piston rod of large diameter, B

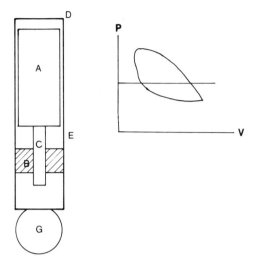

Fig. 5.14 Beal, free piston engine (c.1960)

the heavy piston, D is the hot end with E the cold end of the cylinder, G is the bounce space. Since the mass of the piston is greater than that of the displacer, the displacer will for a given force accelerate faster than the piston. The large diameter of the displacer rod acts as a piston.

Fig. 5.14 also shows the P/V diagram.

The working cycle is as follows. Assume the engine to be at rest in the position shown, heat is now applied to the hot end.

1. The pressure in the engine will rise, in the hot space, and will act on both piston and displacer. The displacer will move more rapidly, so moving more air from the cold to hot end causing a further rise in pressure. Eventually the displacer will meet the piston and they both move together; there is no further flow of gas to the hot end.

2. As the piston moves, the air expands, so pressure falls.

3. Expansion continues until the pressure in the hot end equals the pressure of the bounce space. However, the inertia of the heavy piston is such that the piston continues moving, so causing the expansion of the air to continue. The pressure in the hot space will now fall below that of the bounce space and piston and displacer are decelerated.

4. The displacer being of least mass is the first to respond and moves away from the piston which continues to move down.

5. Air is now moved from hot to cold end, causing the pressure to fall further. The displacer is then rapidly driven back to the top of the cylinder, moving air from the hot to the cold end with further reduction in pressure.

6. The piston halts and is drawn back and the pressure above it rises.

7. The pressure rises to that of the bounce space but by its inertia the piston continues to move and the pressure rises above that of the bounce space.

8. The increase in pressure acts on the displacer which is driven back down to meet the piston.

9. There is no further movement of the air, the pressure rises so retarding the piston. The piston stops, reverses, and the cycle is repeated.

Since there is no physical restraint on the piston it tends to move away from the desired operating point, usually towards to the work space. This is because the pressure wave is not a pure sinusoidal one, but somewhat peaky at the higher pressure end, the result of which is a gradual loss of gas from the working space and the piston creeps towards the hot end. The problem can be overcome by allowing a correcting flow of gas from the bounce space to the working space should the piston move too far.

The free piston engine can, with careful design, be made self starting.

Martini artificial heart (1967)

In a programme sponsored by the United States Energy Commission and the National Heart Institute a nuclear-powered heart was developed by Dr Martini at the Donald W. Douglas Laboratories. A demonstration model was operated in March 1967. Fig. 5.15 shows the engine at rest. The displacer D is held in balance by weights W. A soft spring S helps to keep the displacer in motion. The plug P when in the orifice O separates the gas in the working space from that acting on the pump. When heat is applied the pressure in the working space rises but is constant in the

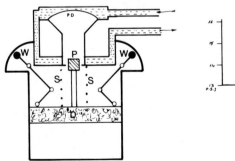

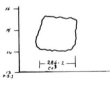

Fig. 5.15 Martini, artificial heart (1967)

pump space. The resultant pressure difference acts on the plug. The plug is pushed up through the orifice, so pulling up the displacer, gas is moved from cold to hot end giving rise to further increase in pressure, and this increased pressure now acts on the pump diaphragm.

The plug having passed through the orifice is restrained by the soft spring, the displacer falls back, gas is moved from hot to cold end and pressure starts to fall.

The plug enters the orifice and is acted upon by the difference in pressure between the two chambers and is pulled down.

The spring acts to slow the motion of the displacer and then reverse the motion. The balance weights acting to cancel out the weight of the displacer force are only applied when the plug is in the orifice O, which serves to keep the displacer oscillating up and down.

The resulting pressure changes are used to move the pump diaphragm PD and force blood through the heat exchanger situated at the top of the cylinder. The regenerator was of 0.05lb of sintered gold wire 0.001in in diameter and the working gas xenon or argon. Indicator diagrams taken from the engine gave a Papin cycle.

Harwell thermomechanical generator

Following a research programme started in 1966, a series of engines using flexible diaphragms were developed by the U.K.A.E. at Harwell. (UK patent 1,252,258, 1971), the engines working through the interaction of vibrating masses:

> The invention provides a Stirling engine comprising hot and cold variable volume chambers inter-communicating through a regenerator, there being incorporated flexible mechanical structure for permitting movement of the walls of the said chambers to provide variation in volume thereof, the flexible structure being capable of repetitive deflection for the life of the engine at the working temperature. Non-positive coupling means side portions of the hot and cold chambers, said side portions being movable by virtue of the flexible structure, the coupling means transmitting force for maintaining reciprocating gas displacement between the chambers, and the operating components of the engine being tuned to resonate in correct phase relationship in response to the forces transmitted by the coupling means.
>
> Preferably each said chamber is formed at least by a flexible wall or walls, which provides the said flexible mechanical structure.

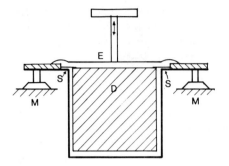

Fig. 5.16. Thermomechanical generator (1970)

Fig. 5.16 gives the general layout of an improved model described in 1974 as capable of delivering 25W AC with an overall conversion efficiency of 13% (11) and in 1982 was reported to have been successfully evaluated by the Department of Trade, being the main power source for a buoy, running for 231 months until the onboard propane tanks ran out (12).

The early diaphragm used to displace the gas has been replaced by a displacer oscillating axially only a few per cent of its diameter.

The machine has two moving assemblies supported by flexible steel suspensions and loosely coupled to one another by the mass of the machine body. The heavy D displacer is suspended from a spring S providing the mechanical coupling to the diaphragm E. The diaphragm is connected to the armature of an electrical generator. The whole mass of the machine is mounted on spring mounts M. The movement of the diaphragm is small, only some 0.5% of its diameter, and to avoid biasing the mean gas pressure on both sides is equal.

The reaction of the unbalanced mass of the oscillating diaphragm and armature assembly induces a small amplitude sinusoidal vibration of opposite phase in the body of the machine (which is supported on standard shock mountings). This movement leads that of the displacer so power is transmitted through the displacer spring, being more than sufficient to maintain the displacer in oscillation.

The mass of the armature and diaphragm centre assembly, and the restoring forces due to the elasticity of the diaphragm and of the working gas, makes the system mechanically resonant. It is heavily damped by the electrical load but not subject to any sliding friction. The phase difference between displacer and diaphragm was found to be between 80 and 90 deg, and this could be varied by changing the mass-loading on the diaphragm-armature assembly which was not found to be critical.

Several other forms of displacer engines have appeared over the years.

The Stirling Cycle is a reversible one, and when a Stirling engine is driven by another prime mover it can act as a heat pump or as an air pump.

Possibly the first successful reversible Stirling engine was made by Alexander Kirk in 1862. Kirk first made a small model with a tin plate displacer cylinder 5in in diameter inside which was fitted a double conical shaped plunger loosely fitting and with a stroke of 1¼in. In the middle of the plunger was fitted a regenerator formed of a number of plates of metallic gauze. The bottom of the displacer formed a conical chamber through which water was circulated to remove the heat from compression. The top of the displacer formed a conical cup into which was placed the substance to be cooled. The whole device was hand driven and Kirk found that he was able to freeze mercury.

Kirk then went on to construct a machine for the extraction of paraffin and he carried this out successfully at the Bathgate Paraffin Oil Works. He also built ice-making machines driven by steam engines, and it is recorded that an ice-making machine working in Hong Kong produced 4lb of ice for each pound of coal (14,15). Kirk with James Young also patented a motive power engine in 1864.

Details of research by the Philips Co into low temperature production of cold can be found in ref. 16.

Another form of driven displacer engine was proposed in 1858 by John Jameson of Gateshead (UK patent 514). This was for an 'Apparatus for Compressing and Expanding Aeriform Fluids'. The machine was to consist of one or more displacer cylinders driven from a crankshaft and heated and cooled in the normal way. Each displacer contained passages running from top to bottom and filled with 'ravellings of fine wire secured therein so as to fill the space while allowing the free passage of air through them, resembling in fact horsehair as it is used for stuffing chair seats etc.' This formed a regenerator. Each cylinder was connected to the next via a non-return valve, each displacer being 180° in advance of the other. When the machine was rotated the pressure in each cylinder was to rise and fall, pumping air from each to the next and finally passing the pressurised air into a reservoir. By connecting the reservoir to the other end of the engine a vacuum could be produced, though Jameson noted that 'Perfect vacuum is manifestly unattainable by this method'.

It is perhaps worth noting that both inventors thought the regenerator a vital working part of their machines.

6

John Ericsson
and the
caloric engine

John Ericsson was born in Vermland, Sweden, the son of a small mine owner. At the age of seventeen he joined the Swedish army and became an artillery draughtsman and land surveyor. Nevertheless he found time to dabble in other fields, inventing and designing machinery, among which were an engraving machine and a model steam engine.

One idea that Ericsson conceived was that a flame might be used in a receiver corresponding to the cylinder of a steam engine. A model was built which seemed to work. In order to seek funds for development of his idea, Ericsson came to England in 1826 with a fellow army officer, Count Adolphe von Rosen. Soon after his arrival Ericsson demonstrated his 'flame engine' with rather disappointing results; in Sweden he had used resinous wood from the local forest but in England he used coal, which gave out a more intense heat and so destroyed the working parts of the engine. These experiments left Ericsson with debts of £1000.

In 1826 Ericsson applied for his first patent (UK patent 5398) for a 'New engine for Communicating Power, to answer the purpose of a steam engine'. The engine was basically a blowing apparatus that fed atmospheric air into a furnace. He left his options open by stating that the heated air from the furnace could be 'led either directly into a cylinder to move a piston for the purpose of communicating power, or it may be led into a boiler to generate steam for that purpose'. Fig. 6.1 gives the layout of the apparatus as given in the patent. The cylinder was fitted with four self-acting valves and to feed coal into the furnace a

system of double doors was to be used. The upper door was opened and coal put into the space between the upper and lower doors, the upper was closed and the lower doors opened and the coal fell onto the fire. Little information is available on Ericsson's early experiments in England, though Church, his biographer, tells us that his next step was to place the fire directly under a piston so as to actuate it by expansion of the air (2). A model constructed to this design was built at his house in 1827, and a second engine was put into operation in Limehouse later in the same year. In this engine the fire was placed at the bottom of an 18in cylinder and through the fire air was forced so as to be expanded by the fire. A loosely fitting piston moved in this cylinder and set in motion a 16in working piston. A brief description is given by Arnot, who states that the experiments showed the effort was found to be several fold greater than that of a steam engine for the same quantity of fuel, but the apparatus was rude and only calculated to prove in a short trial the

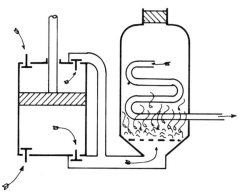

Fig. 6.1 Ericsson, air engine (1826)

129

existence of power, but not the fitness of the machine to endure uninjured, or to be rendered easily obedient to control (3).

In 1827 Ericsson sent to the Institute of Civil Engineers a paper containing a description of his flame engine (1). In his paper he stated that:

> The heat evolved by the combustion, has hitherto alone been employed as a moving power by raising steam, without regard to the nature of the combustibles, and the combustion has always been performed in open furnaces, it has seldom obtained that degree of vividness which is found necessary for obtaining the greatest quantity of heat.

The flame engine was not a success and Ericsson moved away from this design and placed the fire outside the cylinder. In 1828 he met John Braithwait, who was to assist in the building of Ericsson's engine. Their association is best known for their entry in the Rainhill Locomotive Trials, the *Novelty*. At a meeting of the Civil Engineers held in 1853, John Braithwait recalled the first trials of Ericsson's engine:

> There was not any regenerator but there was a separate vessel for heating the air and a refrigerator for cooling it. There was not any difficulty in obtaining power from expanded air but there was great difficulty in finding a lubricator that would enable the piston to work continually as the high temperatures carbonised all the fatty matters that were tried.

The engine was tested by pumping water but the results, he felt, were not equal to those of a steam engine from a commercial point of view.

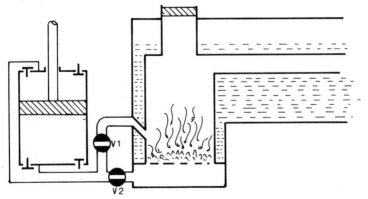

Fig. 6.2 Ericsson and Braithwait, raising steam (1829)

One probable outcome of these early experiments is to be found in a patent granted jointly to Ericsson and Braithwait in 1829 (UK patent 5763) for a 'Mode or method of converting liquids into vapour or steam'. This patent is an improvement on the 1826 patent as a method of forced draught to a fire. The heat of the furnace is controlled by passing air above or under the fire, as shown in fig. 6.2, by means of valves V1 and V2. The idea of forced draught as detailed in the patent was used in an experimental 10hp steam fire pump (also called the *Novelty*) built in 1829 and later in the Rainhill locomotive. This method of controlling power output of a furnace is also to be found in a patent granted in 1837 to Sir George Cayley, but it is not known if Cayley was aware of Ericsson's work.

In his early designs Ericsson had to maintain the air in the working cylinder at a high temperature until the end of the stroke, which led him to seek an efficient means of reducing the heat loss. The solution was his 'regenerator or heat returning apparatus' that transferred the heat from the air, leaving the power cylinder to the air entering it. This design was embodied in his second patent (UK patent 6409) taken out in 1833, for an 'Engine for producing motive power whereby a greater quantity of power is obtained from a given quantity of fuel than heretofore'. In this patent Ericsson claimed that his regenerator would cause 'no continuous consumption of fuel to be required, except what will be necessary to generate heat enough to compensate for losses by radiation and the loss occasioned by the different capacity for heat of the air escaping from and that proceeding towards the working cylinder, so that once a proper temperature has been given to the air, a much smaller quantity of fuel will be sufficient to keep up the motive power of the engine'. A bold claim indeed! He goes on to claim that 'by increasing the density of the air with which the engine is charged, and keeping up the same temperature, increased power to any extent may be obtained'.

It is interesting to note that the description given in the patent is for a marine engine, some time before 1833 Ericsson was involved in conducting trials with the screw propeller. He was aware that steam ships would not be able to compete with sailing ships until there was an improvement in the method of applying steam power, particularly in terms of economy of fuel, and it was not until 1838 that the fastest crossing of the Atlantic by sail was equalled by a steam vessel, the *Great Western*.

In 1827 Robert Stirling, when he was applying for his second patent, met Ericsson and asked him if he confined the air before using it, to which Ericsson replied that he did, but as their plans were quite

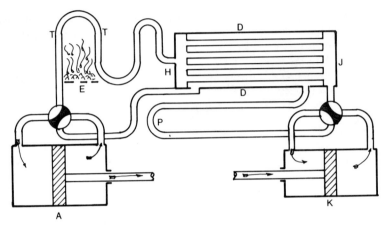

Fig. 6.3 Ericsson, air engine (1833)

different he would not oppose the patent. However, in his biography, Church claimed that Ericsson did oppose Stirling's patent and was greatly annoyed by its claims to priority. Perhaps Ericsson did not know of Stirling's early work.

In 1833 Ericsson exhibited a 'Caloric Engine'. This engine was rated 5hp, and was constructed with a power cylinder of 14in in diameter with a cold cylinder of 10¼in in diameter, both having a stroke of 18in. The engine worked at a pressure of 35psi. With the power checked by a friction brake the engine ran at 56rpm, giving a fuel consumption of 2lb per hp per hour.

Mechanics magazine gave the following description of the machine (fig. 6.3).

> DD is a cylindrical vessel, termed the 'Regenerator', which, in the actual engine, is 7ft 6in long, and 8½in in diameter, fitted with small tubes, which pass through both ends, and terminated in the caps H and J. It also contained a number of division plates, through which these tubes pass, and which plates have segments cut out alternately from their tops and bottoms. These tubes themselves likewise contain a number of small divisions, tapering off towards the centre, each placed in an opposite direction to the other. TT is one of a series of bent pipes, enclosed in a stove E, and acted upon by the fire U; the combustion being supported by the draught produced by a chimney R. The pipes in the stove are all connected with two larger pipes, the one of which communicates with the cap H, and the other, as shown by the diagram, communicates with a four-way cock

attached to the passage-pieces of a cylinder A which is the working cylinder of the engine. P represents one or more pipes, exposed to some cooling medium , and is termed the 'cooler; it contains, also, a number of division plates, similar to those in the tubes of the regenerator, and communicates with the body of the regenerator, as also with the four-way cock attached to the cylinder K.

Ericsson published an explanatory pamphlet on his engine and the following extract is taken from pages 12 to 14:

By keeping the pipes in the regenerator so charged with air as to support a column of mercury 56 inches high, the greatest effort is produced in the trial engine. By the manner in which the slide-valves are worked, the pressure in the body of the regenerator will always adjust itself, so as to support a column of mercury 18 inches high; so that an effective pressure, equal to 38 inches of mercury is kept up. A brake, well oiled and loaded, with 5,000 lbs weight acting on the circumference of a wheel of two foot diameter, fixed on the flywheel shaft, will at the above pressure keep the speed of the engine at 55 revolutions per minute. At this speed 176 cubic feet of heat air, of mean pressure of 17 lbs to the square inch, are admitted into the working cylinder per minute, thereby exerting a force equal to 431,970 lbs moved through the space of one foot: thus $\frac{431,970}{33,000}$ = 13 horse power are communicated to the main crank of the engine. The estimating of this power is, however, of no use other than to give an idea of the amount of friction to which the crank-engine is subjected. In the same space of time, or a minute, 94.6 cubic feet of cold air of a mean resistance of 14 lbs to the square inch, are forced or put into circulation by the cold cylinder, and equal to a resistance of 190,575 lbs moved through the space of one foot. This amount, divided by 33,000 will give 5-7 horses power required to work the cold cylinder – hence the two cranks give and receive the power of upwards of 18 horses. By communicating the power of the hot cylinder to the cold cylinder in a direct manner, the available power, setting friction aside, would be 431,970 – 190,575 = 241,395 lbs moved through the space of one foot. This is equal to $\frac{241,395}{33,000}$ = 7.3 horses power – deducting 2.3 horses for friction would leave 5 horses power. On these grounds the trial engine has estimated at 5 hp. The transferring process has succeeded to such an extent that out of the 10 lbs of fuel which the engine consumes per hour, the product of heat from 3 lbs of fuel only are wasted or carried away by the cooler. This important fact has been ascertained by immersing the cooler in a cistern containing precisely 1081 lbs of water, and by observing the elevation of the ENGINE; and the increase of temperature in that time is not quite 20 degrees – one pound's weight of fuel being capable of raising the temperature of 9,000 lbs of water, it follows that the 1081 lbs contained in the cistern would be raised 8.3 degrees by the combustion of 1 lb of fuel, hence that the actual increase of 20 degrees of temperature is effected by the combustion of less than 3 lbs of fuel. The great discrepancy between the quantity of fuel thus wasted, and that actually consumed by the engine, must be accounted for by the fact, that a considerable extent of radiating surfaces are exposed to the cooling influence of the atmosphere without being surrounded by imperfect conductors.

In practice the regenerator did not live up to theory, experience showing that its advantages were to some extent neutralised by the obstruction offered to the free passage of air. The other difficulty that occurred was in using air heated to 450°F, when oxidation soon destroyed the pistons, valves and other working parts, something that was avoided in Stirling's engine. The engine aroused considerable interest at the time, although some, including Brunel, were not impressed. He found an ally in Michael Faraday, who refused to accept the condemnation passed on Ericsson's theory. When Faraday announced his intention to deliver a lecture on the engine at the Royal Institution a large audience was attracted. But just as he was due to appear on the platform he came to the conclusion that he had made a mistake as to the principle of the expansion of heated air upon which the action of the machine was dependent. To the disappointment of Ericsson he commenced his lecture with an announcement that he was unable to explain why the engine worked at all. Faraday then confined his lecture to the regenerating apparatus, for using heat over and over again in the production of force.

After these experiments Ericsson confined his interest to steam engines and did not build another caloric engine until 1838. This engine was rated at 24 hp and contained a regenerator formed of a box filled with sheets of wire gauze closely packed, and worked well with a small fire but did not keep in order long and was on the whole not very satisfactory. The engine was constructed as a pair with cranks set at right angles, with a large and small cylinder to each engine, and for testing purposes a horizontal double-acting pump, of 3in diameter and 3ft stroke, was coupled up to force water over the top of a 20ft high stand pipe; to give the engine more work to do a loaded valve was fitted to the top (5). This was to be the last engine to be built in England by Ericsson, as he left for America during the following year.

During the American civil war, Ericsson built an ironclad ship, the *Monitor*, for the Union navy, and he also built steam engines, but a large amount of his effort went into improving what he called his 'Caloric Engine'.

Between the years 1840 to 1850 eight experimental engines were constructed, seven of which cost together $9400 and the eighth $7000. Ericsson gradually increased the dimensions from the original 14 to 16 and then 30in, fitted with the new wire mesh regenerator.

'Theory', he said 'clearly indicates that, owing to the small capacity for heat of atmospheric air – that beneficial property which the Great Mechanician gives to it as a fit medium for animated warm beings to live in and, in consequence, also, of the almost infinite subdivision among the wires, the temperature of the circulating air in passing through the regenerator of the caloric engine must be greatly changed. Practice has fully realised all that theory predicted, for the temperature at X and Z (that is, at the points of entrance to and exit from the regenrator) have never varied during the trials less than 350 degrees, when the engine has been in full operation; indeed it has been found impossible to obtain a differential temperature of less magnitude with sufficient fires in the furnace. The great number of discs, their isolated character, and the distribution of the air in such a vast number of minute cells, readily explains the surprising fall and increase of temperature of the opposite currents passing through the regenerator, and which constitutes the grand feature of the caloric engine, effecting as it does, such an extraordinary saving of fuel by rendering the caloric not converted into work active over and over again.

Letters written by Ericsson during this period show that he was at work upon his caloric engine in 1847. Early in December of that year a model engine was sent from the factory and set up in his room at no. 95 Franklin Street for experiment. On 23rd December he wrote: 'The caloric is nearly finished. It will beyond all question succeed. Never felt so sure in my life'.

Six weeks later, 14th January, 'I am at this moment under lock and key with Harrison, who is engaged in the secret operation of stuffing the guts of the regenerator of the caloric, which is in all other respects ready for trial. I have had pressure, and all is tight. The thing must go'.

But not yet, for on 20th January he wrote 'The caloric is not yet complete; a deposit of water, occasioned by the pressure of the atmospheric air within the machine, has given me trouble, great trouble. The steam formed from this water had produced inflammation in the stomach of the regenerator. Cold applications have been resorted to without reducing the undue temperature. All that medical skill can effect will be done, and no fears need be apprehended as to the safety of the patient.'

On the principle that troubles never come singly, Ericsson at this time, as he wrote to another correspondent, 'suffered the pains of the damned' having been obliged to lose three of his back teeth, to cure toothache. A few days later, 27th January, he reported concerning the ailing one, for whom he served as physician, that 'the patient is yet labouring under his intestine complaints, caused by water in the stomach, but his physician entertains strong hopes of a complete cure'.

Then on 2nd February 1848 he wrote:

> I fear the unexpected difficulty cannot be got over without a material change in the apparatus. 'Take nothing for granted' is an excellent precept in all mechanical combinations where the physical agents are called upon to co-operate. Understand me, I have not discovered anything wrong in the principle of the motive power engine, practical difficulties alone have presented themselves in a new quarter. Bent as I am on doing something great in my line, I thank God that I have the vast steam-engine improvement to fall back upon, scarcely inferior in importance, whilst more readily convertible into dollars. So don't be alarmed, we shall still go to London together.

The visit to England was never realised. Five days later on 7th February he wrote:

> I have, after serious reflection, decided on making the requisite alteration in the caloric, the new parts are all on hand and probably in two weeks I start again. The new difficulty I met with took me aback for a day or two, but I feel now as warm and confident as ever – now, don't laugh at me when I tell you 'next time' the thing will go off without a screw to alter. I can hardly be mistaken in supposing that I now see all the difficulties that can have any material bearing on the operation of the great principle in practice. I am shocked to think that for a single moment I should have contemplated relinquishing my gigantic scheme.

Then on 15th February: '. . . the alteration of the caloric was more than half completed, and the inventor was 'in fine spirits and full of confidence'. In another fortnight he was able to announce that all difficulties had been overcome and the caloric engine was ready for trial. On 3rd March he reported, saying:

136

I wrote last Saturday that the caloric engine was ready for trial. So it was, excepting some hard ingredients for its stomach which it does not take five minutes to cram in. Now these ingredients, however simple, the manufacturer did not let me have until last night – confound him! On starting the affair this morning everything went straight off, as I had calculated, and, as you suppose, the thing does everything but talk. I am writing under the click-clack of the machine, and have not time to go into particulars now.

On 18th March: 'Caloric does work', he wrote 'and not a single practical detail remains to be removed'.

By 1851 the work on developing the new motor had advanced to the production of a ninth experimentl engine, costing $17,000. This had a stroke of 2ft and two compressing cylinders of 48in diameter. The regenerator of this engine contained an aggregate of 13,520,000 meshes for each working cylinder, the two thus distributing the air through more than 27 million minute cells, there being, necessarily, as many small spaces between the discs as there are meshes. As there were 228,000ft, or 41½ miles, of wire in each regenerator, the metallic surface presented was claimed to be equivalent to that of four boilers, each 40ft long and 4ft in diameter. The regenerator occupied 2 cu ft compared with boilers that would fill 1920 times that amount of space. After putting a moderate quantity of fuel into the furnace, the engine worked for three hours without fresh fuel, and it frequently worked for

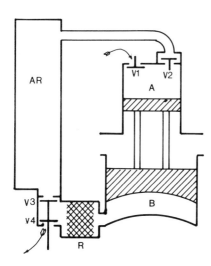

Fig. 6.4 Ericsson, air engine (1851)

one hour after the fires had been drawn. Eleven ounces of fuel were consumed per horsepower per hour. It was estimated that 9oz were required to make good the loss of radiation into the air in contact with the exterior of the machine, the other 2oz being lost in the process of transferring the heat to and from the regenerator.

The engine (fig. 6.4) was made up of the working cylinder B, the supply cylinder A, self-acting valves V1 and V2 and cam driven valves V3 and V4. R is the regenerator and AR an air receiver. The cycle of operation was:

1. With the piston at the bottom of its stroke with V3 closed and V4 open the air receiver is pumped up to a pressure of 8psi.

2. When valve V3 is opened and V4 closed the compressed air acts on the working piston driving it up. Air contained in the supply cylinder is driven through V2 into the air receiver AR.

3. Just before the top of the up stroke V3 is closed and at the top of the stroke V4 opens. The piston now falls and a fresh charge of air is drawn in through V1. The hot air below the working piston is discharged through V4 having first passed through the regenerator R, giving up its heat.

4. At the bottom of the down stroke V4 is closed and V3 opened and the cycle repeated, the cold air passing through R being warmed before final heating in B.

Although the engine worked on an open cycle, by coupling valves V4 and V1 together with pipework, the engine could be converted to a closed cycle.

In 1848, Mr Sargent had suggested that Ericsson should build a 50hp engine for exhibition in Washington. To this suggetion he replied:

I must observe in regard to the caloric that if I had any confidence in justice in Washington I would not hesitate to build the fifty horse-power engine, but, I well know that I am as likely to be cheated as patronised there – you know that too.

In January 1852 the King of Sweden sent to Ericsson his sincere congratulations on the success of his test caloric engine. Of a new venture Ericsson wrote:

The regularity of action and perfect working of every part of the experimental thirty inch engine, completed in 1851, and above all its apparent great economy of fuel, inclined some enterprising mer-chants of New York in the latter part of 1851 to accept my proposition to construct a ship for navigating the ocean, propelled by paddle-wheels actuated by the caloric engine. This work was commenced forthwith, and pushed with such vigour that within nine months from commencing the construction of the machinery, and within seven months of laying of the keel, the 32 foot paddle-wheels of the caloric ship *Ericsson* turned around at the dock. In view of the fact that the engine consisted of four working cylinders of one hundred and sixty eight inches diameter, six foot stroke, and four air-compressing cylinders of 137 inches diameter, and six foot stroke, it may be claimed that, in point of magnitude and rapidity of construction, the motive machinery of the caloric ship stands unrivalled in the annals of marine engineering. The principal engineers of New York all expressed the opinion that a better specimen of workmanship than that present by the huge engines of the caloric ship had not been produced by our artisans at that time.

The *Ericsson* was certainly a singularly bold undertaking, and shows the confidence that her designer could inspire in businessmen in that he should be able to raise the money needed to build her. The principal shareholder was Mr John B. Kitching, a young man of wealth, and another shareholder was Mr Edward Dunham, president of the Corn Exchange Bank of New York.

The cost of the vessel was about half a million dollars, the engines costing $130,000. The length was 260ft, breadth 40ft, and draught 17ft, with the tonnage nearly 2,200. The keel was laid in April 1852, and she was launched five months later, on the 15th September, with the trial voyage on 4th January 1853. It is remarkable that a vessel of a novel design should have been completed in such a short time, a time that was claimed to have been half that ordinarily required to complete a vessel of her class, at that period.

A week after the trial voyage, Tuesday, 11th January, an invitation was given to editors and reporters of all the New York newspapers, Freeman Hunt of the *Merchants Magazine* and according to the *New York Daily Times*, 'a few gentlemen whose scientific abilities render them amply qualified to pronounce judgement upon a project fraught with moment-ous results' (8). There was, however, one uninvited guest, Orson Munn, the 28-year-old editor of the *Scientific American*, who slipped aboard and sounded the only jarring note in an otherwise solid and harmonious praise (9). Munn, a patent lawyer who used his paper's columns to promote the inventions of his clients, had not been invited for the reason that Ericsson felt that he could not expect fair treatment by Munn, Ericsson not being one of Munn's clients (10).

The publicity voyage took the *Ericsson* from the Battery to a point off Fort Diamond in the Narrows, about seven miles distance, and return, the ship being under way for about two and a half hours.

A well-prepared programme or, as the *Scientific American* called it, 'a sort of "sell" played off on the reporters' kept the press occupied. There was breakfast for those who had been hurried by the early hour of departure and wine for those who had not. In the great cabin Ericsson, using a paste-board working model explained 'in a very persuasive manner' how the engine worked and why. The reporters were allowed into the engine room where John Ericsson capitalised on the low speed of his caloric engine by inviting his guests to ride on the open top of the 14ft piston. 'Our sensation on riding up and down on these huge pistons we shall not soon forget' wrote one rider (11).

Finally there was a banquet filled by speeches, toasts and long loud applause. In one speech Professor James P. Mapes, consultant on brewing and agricultural chemistry, and a good friend of Ericsson, declared 'I consider there were but two epochs of science – the one marked by Newton, the other by Ericsson'. To which reports the *Scientific American* 'the inventor to whom this unwholesome flattery was paid rebuked the speaker with manly modesty'. During the trip a committee was drawn up to draft the inevitable resolution praising the virtues of the caloric engine and its inventor. One of these resolutions declared 'that the peculiar adaptability to sea vessels of the new motor presented to the world by Captain Ericsson, is now fully established and is likely to prove superior to steam for such purposes'.

As the party left the ship the irreverent editor Munn piped a 'Vive la Humbug', to which Professor Mapes quickly retorted 'Here's a man proposing his own health' (12).

Next morning the *New York Daily Tribune* declared: 'The demonstration is perfect. The age of steam is closed, the age of caloric opens. Fulton and Watt belong to the past; Ericsson is the great mechanical genius of the Present and Future'.

The *New York Daily Times* referred to the event as one 'which will be held memorable in the ages yet to come'.

The *Daily Times* also reported in detail the question and answer session that Ericsson presided over during the trip. Some explanation of the uniformly laudatory tones of the press is to be found in the reporters' reaction to the inventor's reply. To anyone that might object to the fact that the ship only made 6½ knots (7½mph) while a ship of the Collins Line made 14 knots, it was made abundantly clear that . . . 'it was only intended on this occasion to exhibit the sailing qualities of this vessel; so that this rate of speed should be considered rather as the minimum, than as the maximum of her capability'. There were mechanical imperfections in the engines, admitted Ericsson, but these

Plate 16 Caloric ship *Ericsson*

would be rectified. Besides, the power of the engines could be augmented by increasing the size of the cylinders. He at first wanted to make the cylinders 16ft in diameter, but the constructors would not then attempt so large a casting. Now, said Captain Ericsson, Messrs Hogg and Delameter (the constructors) would be glad to make 20ft diameter cylinders 'at their own risk'. This pronouncement was met by 'great applause'. And when Captain Ericsson said the trial 'had exceeded my highest anticipations' the cabin rang with cheers.

The *Scientific American* totally condemned the principle of the caloric ship and persistently predicted its failure, but its treatment of the trip was on the whole reasonable. Editor Munn noted that 'the designer and constructors of its machinery have shown themselves to have long heads and skillfull hands. We have never seen anything to compare with the castings. It is safe and comfortable for passengers and it saves the fireman from the pandemonium of our steamships'. He did, however, question the competence of the newspaper writers who were present, stating that Ericsson was 'far more modest of what he has done than they are'. He ventured the thought that 'we cannot but think that the good opinion of one eminent practical engineer in favour of the hot air engine would be worth more than all the rest of the daily paper fraternity besides' (7).

Some twenty years after the launching of the *Ericsson*, John Ericsson wrote to the *Scientific American* on 20th July 1875, stating:

> After having completed the general design of the motive engines of the caloric ship, and finding that in proportion to the power

141

exerted by the 72 inch trial engine, a speed of five miles an hour called for cylinders of 168 inches, 6 foot stroke, I hesitated in undertaking the construction. But for the encouragement received from some of our leading commercial men who were consulted on the subject, the caloric ship would not have been built. Let me add, that all united in the opinion that if a speed of seven miles could be produced, the work should proceed. Francis B. Cutting, the eminent patent lawyer, who took a greater interest in the scheme than probably anyone else, stated emphatically during a conversation at the Union Club, that if I felt sure of being able to produce a rate of five miles an hour, I ought not hesitate, reminding me of Fulton and his first attempt. I have never before communicated the above facts to anyone, excepting a few intimate friends; nothing short of my integrity having been assailed in your columns would have induced me to make a statement which I had reserved as an accomplishment to my account of the world's first and last big air-engine.

I abstained in my letter of Saturday, from adverting to your editorial reference to 'the Ericsson hot-air stock-jobbers,' confident that you had inadvertently made the damaging remark.

Replying to a complimentary letter (7th July 1865) from J. B. Kitching, Ericsson wrote:

Your remark about the Caloric ship gratifies me more than I can express. There was more engineering in that ship than in ten Monitors. I regard the hot-air ship as by far my best work, it was simply a mechanical marvel. The four 168 inch working cylinders and four air-compressing cylinders of 137 inch, sink the Great Eastern machinery into insignificance.

The comparison between steam ships of the time and the caloric ship was made by Ericsson's critics. The *Baltic* and the *Pacific* were two ships of the Collins line and each used during a 24-hour period 58 tons of coal; the *Ericsson* consumed six tons during the same period. With this amount of fuel the engines of the *Ericsson* worked at a pressure of 6psi, propelling the ship at 7mph with a possible eight. Critics declared that the difference in speed explained the difference in coal burnt; not so, replied Ericsson. The consumption of coal, he claimed, was nearly all due to radiation; an increase in power and speed would not result in a corresponding increase in coal consumption, and that on a large scale, much of this radiation would be prevented. The question was never tested. Difficulties innumerable assailed the engine, for working at a temperature of 444°F and constantly subjected to the destructive

142

influence of dry heat, lubricants dried out, joints loosened and working parts were destroyed by oxidation.

After being thrown open to the public for a day or two, the *Ericsson* started on a round trip to Washington on 16th February, a distance of some 500 miles. The speed was variously reported as averaging 4·7 to 6 knots, while the public was assured that 'she made no attempt to try her speed on her way hither, that forming no part of the object of the voyage'. The ship was visited in Washington by President Fillmore and a delegation from both houses of Congress. Ericsson convinced the Secretary of State for the Navy, J. P. Kennedy, that a large frigate could be built that would attain 10 knots with a maximum fuel consumption of 8 tons of coal in 24 hours. Accordingly the Secretary asked Congress to appropriate $500,000 to have Ericsson build such a vessel, but met with no success (13).

Kennedy may have been influenced not only by Ericsson's persuasive arguments in favour of his caloric ship but also by a report from his Commander of the US Navy, Joshua Sands.

Washington, Wednesday, Feb. 23, 1853

Sir: I have the honour to acknowledge the receipt of your letter of the 22d inst and in obedience to your instructions beg leave to submit the following brief statement. My object in requesting permission to make a passage in the caloric ship, on her recent trip, was to witness the practical operation of the new motive power; and if it fortunately happened that the weather which we encountered was such as enabled me to satisfy myself on the points with regard to which I had entertained doubts. I was apprehensive that with the new engine it would be impossible to obtain that continuity of action in a seaway which the steam engine has. To my astonishment, however, I found that, during a run of seventy-odd hours consecutively, there was not a single stop in the engine, nor was there the slightest check to the steady movement of the paddle-wheels, although the ship often rolled her weather wheel out of the water, and pitched considerably. I was also apprehensive that the immense size of the piston, and the elevated position of the upper cylinder, would be likely to produce derangement when the ship rolled and pitched heavily. I noticed very carefully that there was not the slightest giving way in any part, everything remaining as firm as if the ship were lying at her dock. The piston moved perfectly steadily and smoothly while the ship was rolling and pitching.

I had heard a good deal said of the great heat applied to the engine, and therefore frequently visited the fire rooms, and found, to my surprise, they were as cool as a cellar. I was much struck with the fact that only one fireman was required on duty at a time, and that he had to supply a small quantity of coal occasionally. I learnt that the regulation was to put in sixty-five pounds every eighty minutes in each of the eight furnaces.

The ship encountered gales or headwinds much of the time from leaving Sandy Hook last Wednesday morning, between 9 and 10 o'clock, until the anchor was let go near the mouth of the Potomac on Saturday, in a snowstorm, it being impossible for the pilot to proceed. The weather was such during the voyage that the canvas could be used to little advantage at any time. My attention was particularly called to the pressure kept upon the engines, which Captain Ericsson strictly limited to eight pounds. The speed during the gale averaged six and a half turns of the wheel a minute: when the wind was moderate the log indicated six to seven knots at sea.

It would be useless to notice particularly the speed, as the working pressure was limited, as I have already stated; at the same time I must say that the result was altogether satisfactory.

On the whole, I deem the test trip of the Ericsson as conclusively establishing the success of the new principle; and I trust the day is not remote when its introduction into our naval service may free our ships from the danger of being blown up by a chance shot through the boiler, perhaps in a very moment of victory.

I have the honour to be, Sir, your obedient servant,
Joshua Sands

Commander United States Navy.

After the caloric ship had returned back to New York, it was decided to make changes in her engines, to increase the efficiency and correct defects. Ericsson, it would seem, had counted too confidently on his regenerator as the heating power of the furnaces was insufficient. Blowers were added to force the drafught and make good deficiencies in the area of grate surface. The *Ericsson* was finally made ready for another trial, and took a trip down New York Bay on 15th March 1854. A second trip followed on 27th April, and the next day Ericsson wrote to Mr Sargent, concerning the results:

At the very moment of success – of brilliant success – fate has dealt me the severest blow I have ever received. We yesterday went out on a private preparatory trial of the caloric ship, during which all our anticipations were realised. We attained a speed of from twelve to thirteen turns of our paddle-wheels, equal to full eleven miles an hour, without putting forth anything like our maximum power. All went on magnificently until within a mile or two of the city (on our return from Sandy Hook), when our beautiful ship was struck by a terrific tornado on our larboard quarter, careening the hull so far as to put completely under water the lower starboard ports, which unfortunately the men on the freight deck had opened to clear out some rubbish, the day being very fine. The men, so far as we can learn, became terrified and ran on deck without closing the ports, and the hold filled so rapidly as to sink the ship in a few minutes. I need not tell you what my feelings were as I watched the destructive element entering the fireplace of the engines, and as the noble fabric, yielding at my feet, disappeared inch by inch. A more sudden transition from gladness and exultation to disappointment and regret is scarcely on record. Two years of anxious labour had been brought to a successful close, the finest and strongest ship perhaps ever built was gliding on the placid surface of the finest harbour in the world and within a few cable lengths of her anchorage; yet, with such solid grounds for exultation, and with such perfect security from danger, a freak of the elements effected utter annihilation in the space of a few minutes.

As it was impossible under these circumstances to demonstrate the capacity of the vessel, a certificate of her performance on the trip that ended thus disastrously was prepared and signed by five persons who witnessed it. They united by saying that the engines of the vessel were worked up to 'twelve turns per minute against quite a strong breeze'. An average pressure of seventeen and one-half pounds was carried in both furnaces, and a mean pressure at the time of closing the cut-off valve of twelve and one-half pounds per square inch. This gave eleven miles an hour through the water, the wheels being thirty-two feet in diameter. The excursion being merely preparatory to a regular trial trip, the consumption of fuel was not ascertained. These witnesses estimated it at a little less than nine tons for twenty-four hours.

In response to a letter of condolence received from Sargent, Ericsson wrote:

You are quite right in thinking that it takes something more to kill me than the sinking of a ship, though it carried down the results of twenty years of labour. I am in abundant pin-money, having brought out some small inventions kept back by the absorbing caloric.

The same day, 1st May, he wrote:

The ship is up, much to the sorrow of numerous wise men who

predicted that the thing could not be done. Pray present my warm thanks to Commodore Smith for the prompt manner in which he ordered his officers to put the ship on the government dock. Gentlemen are so confoundedly scarce in these diggings that it is quite refreshing to me to come in contact with officers of the navy now and then.

Commodore Joseph E. Smith was Chief of the Naval Bureau of Yards and Docks from 1846 to 1869.

After examining the caloric ship, Ericsson reported on 19th May that twelve thousand dollars would be required to put her machinery in order. It was finally decided to take out the *Ericsson's* caloric engines and convert her into a steamer. The *Ericsson* was used during the American Civil War, first as a Government transport and then fitted up with a battery of small guns. She was finally converted into a sailing ship and employed by the British Government in carrying coal to a Pacific station. Though the economy of fuel in hot-air engines was very considerable, it was accompanied by too great a sacrifice of space, and too great an outlay of machinery, to permit competition with the steam engine at its best state.

Each of the four 'regenerators' contained 150 discs of $\frac{1}{16}$ in wire mesh, each disc measuring six by four, or 24 sq ft, contained in a chamber 6ft high by 4ft wide and 1ft thick. As the open spaces in each disc measured half this, or 12 sq ft, there was no appreciable resistance to the passage of air to and from the cylinders, Ericsson tells us. But the great volumes of the vessels containing the wires through which the air passed, from the supply cylinder to the working cylinder, seriously diminished the effective pressure acting on the working piston.

In his centennial volume (p.438) Ericsson said of his vessel:

The average speed at sea proving insufficient for commercial purposes, the owners, with regret, acceded to my proposition to remove the costly machinery, although it had proved perfect as a mechanical combination. The resources of modern engineering having been exhausted in producing the motors of the caloric ship, the important question has forever been set at rest: can heated air as a motor compete with steam on a large scale? The commercial world is indebted to American enterprise – to New York enterprise, for having settled a question of such vital importance. The marine engineer has thus been encouraged to renew his efforts to perfect the steam engine, without fear of rivalry from a motor depending on the dilation of atmospheric air by heat.

Though Ericsson was able in after years to speak so philosophically concerning his defeat in the matter of the caloric ship, we may be sure that the experience at the time was bitter and humiliating.

In the London *Mechanics Magazine*, for 22nd July 1853, there appeared the following:

THE ERICSSON

The fame of Gotham is historic,
Her son's built a ship caloric,
Which would not 'go a-head' at all,
But sank near Jersey in a squall.
The Gothamites, with might and main,
Will try to get her up again;
Some with steam tugs with derricks on
Will raise the humbug Ericsson.
They'd better leave her where she is –
She ain't worth nothing when she's riz!

Ericsson did not publish detailed drawings for the machinery fitted in the *Ericsson*. The layout seems to have followed that detailed in his patent of 1851 (US patent 8481, 4th November 1851). Two sets of working and supply cylinders were fitted forward of the paddle shaft and two sets placed abaft of it. A pivoted horizontal working beam transmitted power from the forward units through a connecting rod to the crank; a second working beam and connecting rods shared a single crank pin.

Atmospheric air was drawn into the upper cylinder as its piston moved downward, and the air was compressed on the return stroke. When a pressure of about 8psi was reached the compressed charge of air was delivered to the receiver. From the receiver the air was led through the regenerator to be preheated before entering the working cylinder, to be further heated by the fire placed below the cylinder. The heated air expanded against the working piston driving it upwards. On the return stroke the air was discharged through the regenerator to impart its heat to the wire screen of the regenerator ready to warm the next incoming charge of air.

In his regenerator, Ericsson perhaps placed too much faith, as the following extract from his 1851 patent shows. The idea seemed good but as he was later to find, what is good in theory is not always easy to prove in practice.

My invention consists in certain improvements in the known principle of producing motive power by the application of caloric to atmospheric air or other permanent gases or fluids susceptible of considerable expansion by increase of temperature, the mode of applying the caloric being such that after having caused the expansion or dilation which produces the motive power the caloric is transferred to certain metallic substances, and again transferred from these substances to the acting medium at certain intervals or at each successive stroke of the motive engine, the principal supply of caloric being thereby rendered independent of combustion or consumption of fuel. Accordingly, while in the steam engine the caloric is constantly wasted by being carried off into the atmosphere, the caloric is in such engines employed over and over again, dispensing with the employment of combustibles, excepting for the purpose of restoring the heat lost by expansion of the acting medium and that lost by radiation; also for the purpose of making good the small deficiency unavoidable in the transfer and re-transfer of the caloric.

Although Ericsson fostered the idea that caloric was trapped within the wire mesh of his regenerator – numbering some 50,000 'minute cells' – and would be given back to the next charge of air passed through it, the reality was something different (15). When the regenerator has reached equilibrium conditions, there would be a temperature gradient across it, the cold end possibly about 120°F while the hot end may have been closer to the operating temperature of about 480°F. Taking into account the specific heats of iron and air, it can be shown that any element of the regenerator would be heated and cooled by successive changes of air by no more than 15°F. Thus the regenerator was of ample size to act as a heat exchanger, but a regenerator could not, even under the influence of Ericsson's sanguinity, seize caloric after it had done work and return it to the engine to be used over and over again. A regenerator might utilise heat that would otherwise be lost, but not heat that has already done work. Ericsson never claimed that he could get more energy from a fuel than it contained, merely that he wanted to utilise the energy in its entirety, pursuing perhaps a will-o'-the-wisp.

Ericsson never published performance figures for his engines that exhibit evidence of their having been obtained from an actual test of the machinery. He seemed to have been unwilling to give actual performance figures or release much data, and when critics began to analyse the performance of the engine using such data as could be found, Ericsson was quick to question the motives, experience, ability and conclusions obtained. Inadvertently he did give some data in his replies to his 'detractors'. For the two-cylinder stationary test engine, built before work was started on the *Ericsson*, the working cylinders were of 6ft diameter with a stroke of 2ft and the output was claimed to be 60hp (16). During a press conference on board the *Ericsson* he gave the power of the engines as 600hp, though various calculations that have been made from available data, give figures ranging from 116 to 316hp (17).

Ericsson later made another attempt to power a ship with caloric engines, when a vessel named the *Primera* was built and fitted with horizontal engines drawing their supply of air from and exhausting into a source of high pressure. However, the heating surfaces proved inadequate and the power produced thus too small; after a short trial steam engines were substituted.

The experience of the caloric ship did not seem to in any way destroy Ericsson's faith in his caloric engine. In a letter to the *London Builder*, dated 23rd April 1853, he claimed:

> The caloric engine is destined ere long, its opponents notwithstanding, to be the great motor for manufacturing and domestic purposes, because of its entire freedom from danger alone. It is destined assuredly to effect much in dispensing with physical toil with the labourer. The artisan of moderate means may place it in his room, where it will serve as a stove while turning his lathe, at the same time purifying the atmosphere by pumping out the impure air and passing it off into the chimney. In time, it will heat, toil, ventilate, and always remain harmless. All this will soon be exhibited in practice and save critics from racking their brains to discover theoretical mistakes and practical imperfections.

However, Ericsson was forced to abandon his efforts to further the development of the caloric engine as a universal motor to supersede steam. He also abandoned the wire regenerator. The truth was that at that time there was not a wire fine enough to give any degree of efficiency and no metal suitable to withstand high temperatures without oxidising, so, as James Stirling had found, high power output from air engines would have to wait for improvements in metallurgy.

Ericsson's feelings at this time are summed up in a letter written by him to his associates, Messrs Stroughton, Tyler and Bloodgood, on 16th January 1855.

> You will not be surprised to learn that for want of means I have after prolonged struggles, at last been compelled to abandon the prosecution of the invention which formed the subject of our several agreements four years ago. Whilst I refrain from dwelling on the painful disappointment I experience in being forced to abandon the grand idea of the wire system which, together with that peculiarly

simple arrangement of inverted cylinders, formed the principle of the improved caloric engine which you joined me in prosecuting, I feel bound emphatically to state my conviction that this extraordinary system of obtaining motive power will some day be perfect.

I repeat now what I stated to you at our first interview, that on the principle of the improved caloric engine under consideration more motive power may be obtained from a mesh of metallic wires of two feet cube than from a whole mountain of coal, as applied in the present steam engine. Every experimental trial made has more realised my anticipations as regards the rapidity and certainty of depositing and returning the caloric on this remarkable system. The practical adaptation alone has presented difficulties. In justice to myself, allow me here to remind you that I have no funds at my disposal for making experiments. The large test engine intended for the London Exhibition was built in all essential features like my original thirty-inch cylinder engine, that being deemed complete, the difference being mainly the application of two pairs of cylinders. The engine of the caloric ship, again, was a perfect copy of the large test engine, differing only in size and in having four instead of two pairs of cylinders. The magnitude of the ship and the consequent heavy responsibility forbade the slightest deviation from the engine which had been found to work satisfactorily. Accordingly, and most unfortunately, not a single point was gained by these undertakings, not a step was made in advance. The small engine built at Springfield indeed established an important fact. It corroborated my opinion that the inverted single-acting cylinder were indispensible to practical success. It has naturally been supposed by the public that I have had ample – enormous – funds at my disposal for making experiments, and hence that the resources of the very principle of the new motor have been exhausted. How utterly at variance with facts are these suppositions! Except as stated in the small Springfield engine, no funds have been expended experimentally, and therefore the improved caloric engine, with its inverted cylinders and wire regenerator, this day stands where it did when you first witnessed the operation four years ago. But though unavailable for practicable purposes it yet rests on immutable physical laws which by money, labour, and patience will assuredly secure a great boon to mankind. There can be little doubt that $50,000, about 10 per cent of the cost of the caloric ship, expended in experiments would teach the proper practical application of the wire system to obtain that available force which so far has not been properly realised.

Truth and candour compel me now to notice that during the four years in which I have laboured unceasingly in a common cause, for a joint benefit, I have been left wholly unsupported by those holding the largest interest in the patent. I have during that period defrayed expenses and incurred liabilities exceeding $30,000 in the prosecution of the patents in which I hold very little more than one-fourth interest. I desire to be distinctly understood not to abandon the invention in which we are mutually interested. I can only stop for want of funds – without money I can do nothing, and my only capital is my intellect and my time. Try what you can do. I am ready to work with all my energies. Only furnish funds, and we will show practically that bundles of wire are capable of exerting more force than shiploads of coal.

In the meantime I find myself on the verge of ruin. I must do something to obtain bread and vindicate to some extent my assumed position as the opponent of steam. Accordingly I am determined to return to my original caloric engine. The plan is less brilliant – less startling – but as it proved to yield power practically twenty years ago, so it will again. At any rate, it cannot fail to be sufficiently useful to save its author from starving. I am sanguine, you know, and I therefore expect confidently to succeed in my old field. If so, I may yet take up the invention in which you have an interest, on the principle which compels metallic threads to yield more force than mountains of coal. Thus I may once more devote individual means and exertions to a common interest.

It says much for the man in that although the caloric ship was a gigantic failure Ericsson, with his determination to make the caloric engine a source of profit, still kept the confidence of his financial backers.

Ericsson went on to build four small engines with 15in cylinders, costing $500 or $600 a-piece and intended for lecture room models; a 16in engine was sent to France, and one of 30in was intended for the Crystal Palace Exhibition in New York. Eight other engines were also built at a cost of $18,000. The end of the year 1857 saw the introduction of the perfected domestic motor with 6 and 8in cylinders, and seven large establishments at work building the new engine.

Next came a 12in machine that proved to be excellent for pumping and light rotary work. This was succeeded by an 18in engine with power sufficient to drive two or three printing presses. Then came a 24in engine capable of doing hoisting work which was claimed to give an increase in power in excess of an increased consumption of fuel. Finally by the end of 1858 an engine of 32in was constructed.

Some idea of Ericsson's line of thought can be gained from a study of

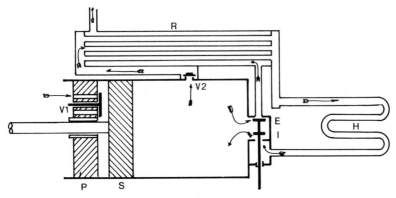

Fig. 6.5 Ericsson, air engine (1855)

three patents he applied for during this period. (US patent 13,348, July 1855: US patent 14,960, April 1856: US patent 22,281, 1858).

The 1855 design is shown in fig. 6.5. P is the power piston, S the supply piston, V1 and V2 are simple self-acting valves, valve E/I is driven from a cam, H is the heater and R a tubular heat exchanger. The cycle of operation was:

1. Starting with P and S at the end of the outward stroke, I is closed and E open. The supply piston is rapidly driven inward by a cam, allowing a fresh charge of air to be drawn in through V2. The air at the back of S is exhausted out via E through R to atmosphere.

2. As S reaches the end of its stroke P moves in to compress the charge of air between S and P so forcing the air out through V2 into R and H.

3. When P has reached the end of its stroke valve E/I changes over and S is rapidly moved toward P so drawing the air through the heater, where it expands, forcing out P on its power stroke, the supply piston S following it.

4. When P reaches the end of its stroke I closes and the cycle is repeated.

The hot air is exhausted through R giving heat to warm the incoming cold air, so giving some measure of economy.

We can see that Ericsson had reverted to his original tubular heat exchanger but had retained the double piston, in a modified form. What is surprising is that he should have persisted with an open cycle engine despite his early experiments with a pressurised closed system engine.

The next move was to experiment with one piston only, retaining the layout of the 1855 machine, fig. 6.6. On the inward stroke air was drawn

152

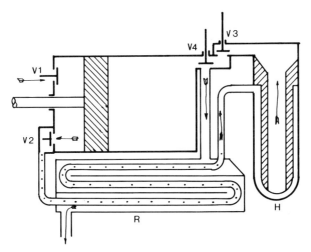

Fig. 6.6 Ericsson, air engine (1856)

into the engine through a self-acting valve V, the air at the back of the piston being exhausted through the regenerator R to atmosphere via a cam-operated valve V4. On the outward stroke of the piston, the air was compressed and forced through a self-acting valve V2, into the regenerator and heater H where the air expands through a cam-operated valve V3 into the cylinder, the power being obtained from the difference in pressure between the compressed cold air on one side and the hot air, acting on either side of the piston.

This attempt at simplification could not have been a success since Ericsson reverted back to the piston layout with a modification that reduced the cam valves to one. The tubular heat exchanger was dispensed with by modifying the design of the supply piston and heater to give an increase in heating surface, the piston skirt acting as a simple regenerator, fig. 6.7.

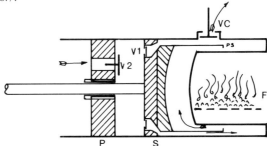

Fig. 6.7 Ericsson, air engine (1858)

Fig. 6.8 shows a schematic layout of the linkwork and a graph of the relative movement of the two pistons.

In the 18in engine the supply piston S, of cast iron, was fitted with a cylinder of thin sheet iron to form a skirt PS. A concave head of sheet iron was inserted in this cylinder and the space between this and the piston was filled with powdered charcoal, or some other non-heat conducting substance, to act as a heat shield. A light iron plate with an annular opening for valve V1 was bolted to the face of the piston, the valve being formed of a thin steel plate placed on the inside and held in place by two flat steel springs. The supply piston worked through the movement off the working piston P, being driven from the crankshaft via a long connecting rod coupled to a rocking lever, a shorter lever connecting the crosshead to the centre of the rocking shaft. This arrangement imparted rapid movement to the supply piston on the suction stroke. The working piston was made airtight by means of a leather packing and was fitted with two circular steel valves opening inwards but kept closed by means of counterweights V2, motion being transmitted to the crank by means of a rocking shaft and levers.

The two pistons moved in a cast iron cylinder open at one end but closed at the other by an enclosure that contained the furnace F, the fire bars being placed within and a heavy cast iron lining placed above to protect it from the action of the fire. The whole of the hot end of the cylinder was contained in a further, double walled casing lined with plaster of Paris to lessen radiation; this casing guided the spent gases from the fire around the cylinder before being discharged up the chimney. The mode of operation was as follows:

1. At the end of their strokes the two pistons move closer together. At the end the internal pressure is still higher than atmosphere due to

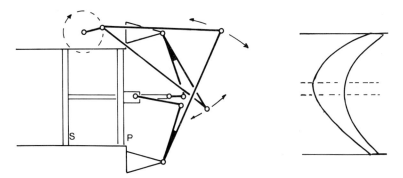

Fig. 6.8   Ericsson, linkwork (1858)

154

incomplete expansion.

2. The exhaust valve VC is lifted by the cam, and the pistons start their backward stroke, the supply piston moving first then the working piston. The valve on the supply piston is held closed while the valves on the power piston open as a fresh charge of air is drawn in. Simultaneously the hot air is discharged through the exhaust valve, and in doing so it circulates past the piston skirt, heating it up.

3. When the supply piston has completed 90% of its stroke, the exhaust valve closes, the inlet valve then falls closed and the cold air is compressed.

4. The supply piston now moves rapidly towards the working piston, the non-return valves V1 open and the cold air is displaced into the hot end. In doing so it passes over the piston skirt and is warmed, being finally heated by the fire. The air is heated and the pressure increased, and since the valves on the supply piston are open no work can be done but the air is free to act on the working piston, so driving it out.

The inrush of cold air with every stroke kept the cylinder and piston cool, the temperature never rising above that which a hand could endure. The engine could be stopped by holding open the exhaust valve and speed control was obtained by bleeding off air via a small valve fitted in the top of the cylinder, the valve being controlled by a centrifugal governor, driven by bevel gears off the crankshaft. On the smaller range of engines starting was effected by pulling round the flywheel, but on the larger machines a series of notches were put in the flywheel rim, so that by means of a lever and pawls the engine could be barred round. A full description with detailed working drawings can be found in ref. 18. The following data has been compiled from various tests on this engine.

Cylinder dia. ins	Stroke ins	RPM	Power		Mech. eff. %
			BHP	IHP	
8	3·9	101	0·13	0·06	27
8	3·9	94	0·2	0·06	30
8	3·9	110	0·27	0·08	29
18	—	37	—	0·7	46
24	18	—	—	—	—
32	—	—	—	—	—

The improved engine was an immediate success and within three years over 3,000 machines had been sold. It was also a financial success;

Plate 17 Ericsson caloric engine

Plate 18 Ericsson duplex engine

156

altogether Ericsson had expended about $60,000 upon 25 experimental engines before perfecting his design, but more than half of this sum was received in the first year in patent fees. One field into which the engine was generally introduced was for driving printing presses, for which the normal power source was a steam engine, but because of the risk of boiler explosions a police licence was required, something not required for a caloric engine.

Over the years many improvements suggested by practical experience were introduced. During the 1860s the engines were manufactured by Jas. A. Robinson, 164 Duane Street, and 136 Reade Street, New York. In his 'Contributions' Ericsson said of the steam engine:

> Steam engineers, finding by the extraordinary demand for caloric engines that very moderate power was a great desideration, have perfected the steam-motor until it almost rivals the caloric engine in safety and adaptability; consequently, the demand for caloric engines has been greatly diminished of late. Yet this motor can never be superseded by the steam-engine, since it requires no water, besides being absolutely safe from explosions. There are innumerable localities in which an adequate quantity of water cannot be obtained, but where the necessities of civilized life call for mechanical motors; hence the caloric engine may be regarded as an institution inseparable from civilisation.

In a letter addressed to the Editor of *The Times* dated 23rd May 1860, Ericsson praised the virtues of his caloric engine:

> The close observer of labour saving machines is well aware that of late years the legitimate bounds have been passed, and that we are rapidly encountering the dangers of intellect-saving machines, by introducing devices for effecting everything which hitherto has been the result of the healthful combination of intellect and muscular effort. At this moment hundreds of thousands of human beings are employed in working a treadle or turning a crank, vacant spectators of what their muscles effect; not the least tax on their intellect. Unfortunately, the number of persons thus occupied is being augmented with a rapidity only known to those who study the records of mechanical invention. It is needless to speculate on the effect upon our race which this dispensing with intellect, and the substitution of monotonous manual labour, will produce in the course of time. The evil is manifest.
>
> It will be asked, 'is there no remedy?' A motor of such properties that it can follow the thousand mechanic denizens into their corners

would obviously meet the difficulty. It is claimed that the caloric engine possesses these properties. It works as well when made to exert the power of one man as that of twenty. It is actuated by the air of the surrounding atmosphere and requires no engineer; it can be managed by any person of common intelligence; is wholly free from danger; the cost of fuel which it consumes amounts to less than five per cent of the manual labour employed to exert equal force. The steam engine requires water which prevents its use in millions of instances in which we want motors to relieve human drudgery. We cannot trust that dangerous agent to the care of our wives and children, but the caloric engine we safely may. We may turn the key to the room which contains it, and the humble artisan may, without apprehension, ply his tool while this harmless servant turns the crank and cooks his food.

Engineering aside, Ericsson seems to have been pleased with what he saw as the social implications of his new power source. In 1865 he wrote:

The satisfaction with which I place my head on my pillow at night, conscious of having through my little caloric engine conferred a great boon in mankind – though the full implications of that boon will not be understood until the lapse of perhaps another century – is far greater than any satisfaction the production of an engine can give.

Although the 1856 design was a commercial success Ericsson seems not to have been too happy with the mechanics. In a patent taken out in 1860 (UK patent 2110) he states: 'In all air engines operated under condensed pressure, as hitherto constructed, the motive force of the working piston has been insufficient owing principally to the rapid diminution of the acting pressure of the air by its expansion during the movement of the piston from end to end of the cylinder'. The design follows the 1856 engine but modified for the use of compressed air, fig. 6.9. A and B are what Ericsson termed 'Equilibrium cylinders' and connected to either end of C which acts as the working piston, connected at the centre by a crosshead and side rods to a crank. V1 and V4 are valves that open when the piston moves to the left and V2 and V3 are valves that open when the piston moves to the right. V5 is a valve that allows the left-hand side of A to communicate with the heater when A is moving to the right and with the cooler when it is moving to the left. V6 operates in a similar manner for piston B. H is the heater, E is the heat exchanger. R is a box full of wire gauze and F the cooler.

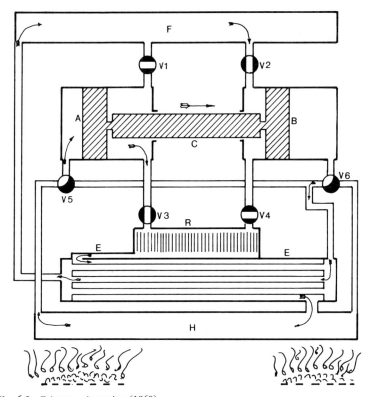

Fig. 6.9 Ericsson, air engine (1860)

Before starting, the engine is first charged with compressed air. To understand the working of the engine consider the piston to be moving to the right. Air on the right-hand side of A will pass through R, E and H to the left-hand side of A, so becoming heated and increasing in pressure. Air on the right-hand side of B will pass through E and C so becoming cooled and diminish in pressure. There will now be a pressure difference across C which will be driven to the right. At the end of the stroke the valves change over and the cycle is repeated; side B will now increase in pressure and A diminish and C will be driven to the left.

As cool air moves from E to H it picks up heat in E and the hot air moving through E to F will lose heat, being finally cooled by F. The regenerator was multitubed as in the 1833 engine, and the purpose of R was to prevent the ingress of hot air into the cold end of the cylinder

159

due to the difference in pressures when V3 and V4 change over. The wire gauze taking up the heat as the air passes through it effects an equalising of pressure, the heat being passed back as the cold air moves towards the heater. To stop the engine valve S is opened, so equalising the pressure across E. This design does not seem to have been made commercially.

In 1864 Ericsson turned his mind to the problem of solar power, but found his caloric engine unsuitable for adaptation to solar heat, as indicated in the following letters:

New York, October 22 1873, 8pm.

Dear Harry,

The world moves – I have this day seen a machine actuated by solar heat applied directly to atmospheric air. In less than two minutes after turning the reflector towards the sun the engine was in operation, no adjustments whatever being called for: in five minutes maximum speed was attained, the number of turns being far too great to admit of being counted.

Having found, by long experience, that small caloric engines cannot be made to work without fail on account of the valves getting out of order, the above solar engine is operating without valves, and is therefore absolutely reliable.

As a working model, I claim that it has never been equalled; while on account of its operating by a direct application of the sun's rays it is marking an era in the world's mechanical history. You shall see it in good time. The two cylinder caloric engine, to be operated by iron where molecules have been put into violent motion, you will be invited to see very shortly.

Yours truly
J. Ericsson.

On 26th December 1873, Ericsson wrote to Mr James Robinson saying:

I omitted to state, when you called to-day, that the successful operation of some of my solar engines in which atmospheric air transmits the energy of the solar heat, some time ago induced me to apply similar mechanism to my caloric engines. I accordingly applied the new movement to a 24 inch caloric engine cylinder and heater. The result was greatly increased speed, but not any gain in actual power developed, as ascertained by the friction brake. I am not willing, however, to abandon my new scheme, although no longer quite sure of success.

160

Adapting another form of my solar engine to a small domestic motor promises better results. I am experimenting with a large model engine which, up to a certain power, has done well. At any rate, it afford me delightful occupation during the hours not devoted to solar observations, torpedoes, amphibic projectiles, monitors, air compressors, turreted gunboats, cavalry cannon, etc.

The new engine worked in the same way as Stirling's machines, with a displacer and power piston. It would seem that Ericsson was averse to patenting his new engine as it formed part of his solar apparatus. In a letter dated 23rd September 1872 he wrote:

I shall not apply for any patent rights, and it is my intention to devote the balance of my professional life almost exclusively to its completion. Hence my anxiety to guard against legal obstructions being interposed before perfection of detail shall have been measurably obtained.

However, pressure from his business associates led him to patent the design in 1880 (UK patent 3086) giving the patent rights to the firm of Delameter & Co. Within a few years many thousands of machines had been sold, mainly for pumping water, yielding profits several times in excess of the $100,000 that Ericsson had spent on his experiments in solar power, from which the engine evolved.

Writing to his son Hjalmar in August 1880, Ericsson said of his new engine:

It is a true copy of the sun motor when steam is not used, the gas taking the place of the concentrated solar heat. It has been so well received here that Delameter's large works are unable to build as fast as orders are coming in.

Two examples of the new engine were exhibited at the London Building Exhibition of 1881. Built by Thomson Sterne & Co. of Glasgow, the engines were of two sizes, 8in and 12in (22). The smaller engine was a nominal ¼hp capable of lifting 350 gallons per hour to a height of 50ft, giving an output of 0·0884hp. The larger was rated a nominal ½hp, being capable of lifting 800 gallons of water to a height of 50ft for the same expenditure of gas, giving an output of 0·202hp. Of these engines *T. Engineer* said . . . 'Taking the consumption of gas at 30 cubic feet per hour for the smaller engine, Mr Ericsson's latest child cannot be said to perform its work with any approach to economy' (21).

A sectional view of the machine is given in fig. 6.10. By arrangement of the crankshaft, the centres of motion of the beam A and bellcrank

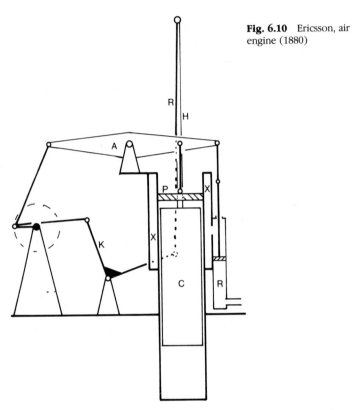

Fig. 6.10 Ericsson, air engine (1880)

lever K and of the connections, Ericsson obtained a short stroke power piston P and a long stroke for the displacer C, and the slight deviation from a straight line made guide rods unnecessary. The side rods R connected the bellcranks to the displacer connecting rod H. The water pump R was connected to an extension of the walking beam. The large surface area of the displacer was designed to act as a regenerator and cooling was obtained by passing water from the pump through a water jacket X before being discharged.

Although the new motor was very successful as a water pump, it was never used as had been originally intended, as a sun motor, although a simpler method of concentrating the sun's rays was later perfected. In a letter to the journal *Nature*, published on 2nd August 1888, Ericsson wrote:

It will be proper to mention that the successful trial of the sun motor attracted the special attention of landowners of the Pacific coast, then

162

in search of power for actuating the machinery needed for irrigation of the sunburnt lands. But the mechanical details connected with the concentration at a single point of the power developed by a series of reflectors, was not perfected at the time; nor was the investigation relating to atmospheric diathermancy sufficiently advanced to determine with precision the retardation of the radiant heat caused by increased zenith distance. Consequently no contracts for building sun-motors could then be entered into – a circumstance which greatly discouraged the enterprising Californian agriculturists, prepared to carry out forthwith an extensive system of irrigation. In the meantime, a simpler method of concentrating the power of many reflectors at a given point had been perfected, while retardation of solar energy caused by increased zenith distance had been accurately determined, and found to be so inconsiderable that it does not interfere with the development of constant solar power during the eight hours called for.

The new motor being thus perfected, and first-class manufacturing establishments ready to manufacture such machines, owners of the sunburnt lands on the Pacific coast may with propriety reconsider their grand scheme of irrigation by means of sun-power.

But the grand scheme was not to be, as John Ericsson was to die within seven months of writing this.

The sun motor was first built by the Delameter Iron Works, New York, and later by the Rider-Ericsson Engine Co., who were the successors to the Delameter Iron Works and the Rider Engine Co. An 'improved' model was also built by the American Machine Co. as the Denny-Ericsson engine.

The following data were compiled from a Delameter Iron Works catalogue of 1890:

Dia. of piston	Overall size		Fuel consumption per hour		Water pumped 50ft high galls/hr	Price with furnace	
	Floor space	Ht	Gas cu ft	An'cite lbs		Coal	Gas
5″	26×14″	48″	15	—	150	—	$150
6″	41×20″	53″	18	24	300	$210	$200
8″	48×21″	65″	25	3⅓	500	$300	$235
10″	50×30″	73½″	—	6	1000	$300	—
12″	54×27″	72″	—	8	1500	$450	—

A Rider-Ericsson engine, built in 1907 and measured by the author was found to have the following dimensions:
Diameter of piston 8in, stroke of piston 4in, stroke of displacer 8½in, diameter of flywheel 29in, overall height 63in. It was coal-fired. The engine itself required little attention or maintenance to keep it running. The following extract is taken from a booklet entitled Directions for Setting and Running the Improved Reeco Ericsson Hot-Air Pumping Engine, built by the Rider Ericsson Engine Co.

Gas-pipe and operation of burner

In setting up the engine with a gas furnace, it is advisable to have the gas-pipe sufficiently large, in order to keep the pressure of the gas up to its proper point when it is delivered to the burners, otherwise the burners will not work satisfactorily. The proper size pipe is ½ inch for 5-inch and 6-inch engines; ¾ inch for 8-inch and 10-inch engines. These sizes will answer unless the pipes are long, when they should be increased.

Connect the burner with gas-pipe and put a cock in the gas-pipe within one foot of engine. Regulate the supply of gas by opening the cock until the proper flame is obtained. There are two holes in the neck of the burner and two corresponding holes in the movable slide on the brass nipple. When lighting the gas or turning it off, the proper position of this movable slide is with the holes in the gas burner neck covered by the solid part of the slide and sufficiently opened to admit the proper quantity of air to have the gas burn with a blue flame.

The right heat is obtained from a blue flame and the engine should start in from ten to thirty minutes after lighting the gas. A little observation of the flame will teach the attendant how to regulate the flame so as to start the engine in the shortest time.

Stove-pipe and draft

A good draft is necessary, particularly when burning coal. The proper size pipe is 5 inch for 5, 6 and 8-inch engines, and 6 inch for 10-inch engine. For burning wood it is not necessary to have the draft so sharp as for burning coal. The best coal to use is anthracite, chestnut size. If the engine is to be placed away from the house and a small house built over it, the stove-pipe should run up about 10 feet, more or less, depending upon the nature of the surrounding objects, such as trees and other houses. The object is to secure a good draft at all times and to have nothing interfere with it, no matter in what direction the wind may blow.

A DAMPER MUST BE PUT IN EVERY STOVE-PIPE.

Firing

COAL. The fire should be THIN and BRIGHT. Too much coal should not be put on at once, but rather a small quantity and often. This will keep the fire at a uniform heat and the engine at a uniform speed. Do not overheat the bottom of the engine. This may be determined by looking through the fire door and shading the light of the fire from the bottom of the engine by a shovel or something of that kind. This part of the engine should not be heated above a DULL RED HEAT.

WOOD. Any kind of wood may be used, and it is difficult to damage the machine with a wood fire.

We furnish special directions for attaching and using burners to use kerosene or gasolene.

Speed

The best speed to run these engines is at 100 to 120 revolutions per minute for the 5-inch and 6-inch engines, and about 80 to 110 revolutions per minute for the 8-inch and 10-inch engines.

Oiling

All the working parts of these machines need a few drops of oil every time the engine is run. Do not use much oil on the cylinder. A swab is furnished with every engine and should be used for oiling the inside of the cylinder instead of applying the oil from a squirt can. A few drops of oil should also be put round the *transfer piston rod* where it works through the leather packing.

OIL. Special oil for use in these engines can be obtained from us, and we advise our customers to send here for the oil they use. If, however, it is too far to send to us for this oil, a mixture of one part sperm oil with two parts of good paraffin oil will answer if used sparingly.

Starting

Start the engine as soon as it is hot enough to run. Be particular about this, otherwise the engine will be unduly heated, and perhaps damage done. While the engine is running the heat developed by the fire is being utilized to heat the air in the machine; but while the engine is standing this is not going on; and consequently the danger of overheating is much greater than when the engine is running. To start the engine, turn the wheel by hand in such a direction that the top of the wheel will turn FROM the top of the cylinder. If the engine is hot enough to run it will only be necessary to turn it by hand about two revolutions, when it will go without no more assistance. *The blow-off cock should be left open while the engine is being heated up, in order to expel any moisture, etc., that may have collected inside the cylinder* while the engine has been standing idle. Shut the cock when the main piston is at the top of its stroke.

Stopping

To stop the engine, open the blow-off cock on the side of the cylinder and, unless the engine is very hot, it will stop after making three or four revolutions. This cock should be left open until it is desired to start the engine again. The engine should not be stopped for any length of time when the fire is burning brightly underneath it. If it becomes necessary to keep the engine standing, cover the fire over with a little fresh coal and leave the fire door partly open, so as to protect the bottom of the engine from becoming unduly heated. The engine should be turned, after it has stopped, to such a position that the transfer piston will be at the top of its stroke, and left standing so until it is started again.

Packing

The packings of these engines are leather and consist of one large packing in the main or air piston and one small or cup-shaped packing on the transfer piston rod. To put on a new air piston packing it should be first well soaked in oil and then thoroughly worked in the hands until it becomes soft and pliable. Remove the air piston from the engine, take off the old packing and replace it with the new one with the flesh side of the leather upward and screw all the bolts down securely. Place the air piston at the top of the cylinder and work the edge of the leather down into the cylinder, being careful to avoid any puckers or unevenness which would allow air to escape. This operation requires only a little care to do it successfully.

The packing of the transfer piston rod is pressed in a mould to the proper shape. Do not oil this packing before putting on. Screw it over the threads on the end of the transfer piston rod with the raised side upward. After passing the threads, unscrew the packing, remove it, reverse it and screw it down to its proper position, then oil it. This method insures the packing fitting tighter and lasting longer.

The pump rod packing is also moulded to the proper shape and has a raised centre. The same method of putting the pump rod packing on should be followed and no oil is needed.

We keep these packings on hand and can supply them at once.

Cleaning

When the engine shows signs of weakness it is frequently because the inside of the cylinder has become foul by too much oiling or from the use of improper oil. As a scale thus formed on the inside of the cylinder and on the outside of the transfer piston is hard it must be removed by

166

scraping and care should be taken to remove all of the scale and dirt that falls into the bottom of the heater. Care should be also taken not to damage the surface of the cylinder of the transfer piston by scraping into the iron. In replacing the transfer piston see that it is properly adjusted by the nuts on the top of the transfer piston rod so that it does not strike on the down or up stroke. To properly adjust the transfer piston, turn the wheel until the side rods are at the highest point, then draw the transfer piston up until it touches the bottom of the air piston, drop it about a quarter of an inch and set it at that point, with the nuts on the top of the rod.

Heater

If the heater should be cracked it becomes apparent through the air blowing through it down into the fire. The heater should be renewed at once, or the transfer piston may be destroyed. To put on a new heater, first remove the furnace; take off the old heater. Make the joint between the cylinder and heater tight, by using red lead mixed with oil and spread it evenly and thin all round the recess in the top of the heater. Screw up all the bolts evenly by tightening up on opposite bolts and go all over bolts two or three times to make sure that they are tight. Before replacing the furnace try whether or not the joint is tight by turning the wheel backwards about half a revolution so as to put a little compression on the air in the machine and while this pressure is kept in the engine examine the joint carefully and listen for any leak. This must be perfectly tight.

Leaks

These engines must be air-tight, or they will not develop the maximum power. They are frequently run however with a leak in the air piston packing, but it is a bad practice to run them so, and when a leak develops itself, a new packing should be put in at once. The *transfer piston should also be perfectly air-tight; that is, the piston itself.* If for any reason, such as overheating or damage from any cause, it leaks air, the engine will not run, and *a new one will have to be put in before the engine will develop its power.*

Conclusion

Be particular to keep the engine CLEAN. Wipe off every time it is used, and before it cools. Allow no slovenly or careless person to take charge, or have anything to do with the engine. Do not think that because it is harmless it requires no attention. Follow these directions carefully and you will always have a willing servant – one that will serve you faithfully, and give you little trouble and anxiety.

7 / Compression engines

All the engines described in preceding chapters can be categorised into one of the following types.

1. Stirling type, having a single piston and separately heated and cooled displacer vessel. Both sides of the piston can be utilized by having two separate displacer vessels so making the engine double-acting.

2. Cayley type, two loaded pistons of unequal diameters running 180 deg apart, stroke of both pistons equal, most used in furnace gas engines.

3. Ericsson type, fitted with a power piston and transferrer piston both fitted with valves.

4. Single piston engine fitted with valves, which falls into two types:

(a) Trunk piston type, where the effective area above the piston is smaller than that below the piston – the equivalent of using two pistons of unequal diameters as in 2.

(b) Movement of the piston within the cylinder such that the volume on the cold side of the piston is greater than that on the hot side of the piston, this effect is also achieved by building dead space into the cylinder as in Wenham's engine.

In all these machines the power stroke operates over only part of the cycle for one revolution. Power was usually increased by coupling up several engines at different phase angles. An alternative to this is to have a multi-cylinder engine giving a continual power stroke.

The term 'Compression Engine' was used to describe a class of engine distinct from those discussed above where 'a given quantity of air is constantly changed in volume, being compressed when cold and expanded when hot' (1).

The first engine of this type seems to have been proposed by a French engineer, Charles Louis Felix Franchot.

Franchot began by first designing an air engine the operation of which had some analogy with that of Ericsson's engine of 1833, only using an open cycle instead, the heated air after acting on the power piston being exhausted under the grate of the furnace.

Franchot then went on with a change of design to develop a displacer type of engine for which he was granted a number of patents:

Brevet D'Invention	No. 11,511	27/12/1838
addition		1/ 3/1839
,,		1/ 7/1839
,,		17/ 8/1839
,,		21/ 8/1841
UK patent	No. 10,427	1844

During 1841 and 1842 Franchot had constructed by a M. Philippe, a Paris engine maker, in conjunction with a young English engineer by the name of Codner, an engine that gave a power output of 4hp for a consumption of 9lb of coke per hour. The project was abandoned after an accident, when the displacer, made of thin cast iron, was unfortunately broken as the engine was being stripped down.

Franchot made a further design change and developed the compression engine which he patented:

Brevet D'Invention	No. 9218	21/2/1853
addition		12/5/1853
UK patent	No. 793	1853 (April)

This new design was for a multi-cylinder engine designed to give a smooth delivery of power continually through one revolution. Each piston acted both as power piston and compressor. The first design, fig. 7.1, used valves to control the movement of air from cylinder to cylinder and worked on an open cycle. On the down stroke of the first piston P a fresh charge of air was drawn into the engine, through V1; on the following up stroke the air was compressed into the next cylinder, via V2 under piston P2 where it was heated and expanded and so drove up the piston forcing the cold charge of air above it into the next cylinder under piston P3. This would be repeated according to the

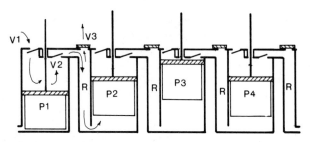

Fig. 7.1 Franchot, air engine (1853)

number of cylinders fitted until cylinder P1 is again reached. The air is exhausted through V3 after passing back through the regenerator R. The pistons were to be of equal diameter, each 90 deg in advance of the other, the engine developing power due to the effect of the differing phase angles of each succeeding cylinder. The velocity of each piston would be greater or less in relation to adjacent pistons.

Franchot then simplified the design by omitting the valves and using a closed cycle as fig. 7.2 shows. This is taken from his UK patent of 1853. R is the regenerator and P the two pistons 90 deg out of phase. In the French patent a four-cylinder engine with pistons of equal diameters in the form of fig. 7.1, without the valves, is described. Franchot gave the following description:

> It will be seen that in this arrangement, first the distributing valves are dispensed with, and that consequently there is no diminution of pressure and shock, which always result from the opening of the passages and the passage of a compressed fluid into a chamber in which only a moderate pressure exists. Secondly, that nevertheless the motive force produced by the hot piston is greater than the power exerted by the cold piston, for by reason of the expansion of the air the hot piston can have a greater section than the cold piston; or if the hot and cold volumes generated be equal the pressure will be greater in the direction of the course of the hot piston than it was in the direction opposite to that of the cold piston; and, moreover, there remains an excess of pressure favourable to the return of the cold piston. Hence it will be seen that the exact proportion between the volumes generated and the dilation by heat is not necessary.

Franchot made a point of stressing the importance of wire gauze regenerators, the advantages of which he had first proposed in 1838.

A model of one of these engines was exhibited at the Paris Exhibition of 1855 where it attracted much interest. In this machine the cranks

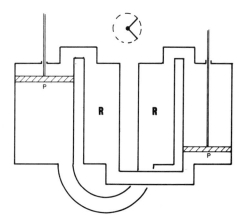

Fig. 7.2 Franchot, compression engine (1853)

were set 90° apart and connected to double acting pistons moving in two cylinders that communicated via regenerators.

A very similar design to that of Franchot was proposed by Charles William Siemens in 1860. Working on an internal combustion cycle, Siemens' engine had evolved from a number of patents granted to him for regenerative steam engines:

UK patent 11,021	1845
12,006	1847
12,531	1849

Although all of Siemens' patents were for improvements to steam engines, in a patent granted to him in 1852 (no. 326) there was a change in design that led him to claim that the engine could be worked with steam or air. In this engine the bottom of the power cylinder was to be heated by a furnace, that also raised steam in a boiler, to between 600-800°F. A charging piston was also fitted, running 90 deg in advance of the power cylinder. The purpose of this charging cylinder was first to receive steam from the boiler and then compress the steam into the working cylinder where expansion would take place.

Improvements in this engine appear in a patent granted in 1856 (no. 1363), mainly for modifications to the heating vessels and the use of a wobble plate drive.

Further improvements were made in a patent granted in 1860 (no. 2074). Instead of using a coal fire to heat the cylinders the coal was to be used instead to produce gas that would then be used to give a more uniform and controllable heating of the cylinders. The charging cylinder was discarded and two or more working cylinders were now made double-acting by closing the ends of the cylinders.

Siemens gave the following description:

Now one of the objects of the present invention is, to improve upon this arrangement by suppressing the third or charging cylinder which produces no direct useful effect, and by adding two or more working cylinders, which are to be attached with their working pistons to two points of the oscillating disc at right angles with those of the two other working cylinders. The four working cylinders are closed in front, and communications are established from the front end of the first to be heated or back end of the second through a regenerator or respirator from the front of the second to the back of the third, from the front of the third to the back of the fourth, and from the front of the fourth to the back of the first named working cylinder, thus completing the circle. In this way the front part of one cylinder answers the purpose of charging cylinder to the next, and so on.

By this improved arrangement the available power of the engine is greatly increased, the motion produced is more uniform, and the losses of heat by leakage and radiation from exposed surface is reduced. This four-cylinder arrangement may be greatly varied in form; instead of attaching the four pistons to four equidistant points on an oscillating disc, they may be attached to the four-throw crank or to two cranks at opposite points of the shaft, upon each of which cranks two working cylinders, placed at right angles to each other, are made to act, or the four working cylinders may be placed radially round a central working crank. The supply of fresh steam or other elastic fluid to the four working cylinders and their partial discharge at the proper intervals of each stroke may be advantageously effected by a rotating valve, with four radial apertures leading to four cylinders and two apertures endways, the one communicating with the boiler or reservoir of elastic fluid in a state of compression, and the other with the atmosphere or a condenser, while the rotary plug is pierced with two apertures divided by an oblique partition . . .

When using air as the working fluid expansion of the air has to be by injecting, by means of a force pump, an explosive mixture of gas and air into the cylinder by means of valves set into the top of each cylinder. This mixture was to be ignited by a form of hot tube ignition and a portion of the spent gases exhausted through exhaust ports exposed as the following piston rose to the top of its stroke.

Fig. 7.3 shows the basic layout of the engine less the necessary valve work. A is the gas compressor worked from one of the cranks, P1-P4 are the four plungers and R the regenerators, C the coolers, V1 an inlet valve, V2 an exhaust valve. The need for a mechanism for admitting and exhausting gases makes Siemens' design a less elegant design for obtaining power when compared with the earlier design by Franchot. However, Siemens' use of the wobble plate drive does lead to a more compact layout.

There seems little evidence to show that a working multi-cylinder engine functioning on an external combustion cycle was built after Franchot's engine until the design was taken up by Philips in Holland in the 1940s. Philips' engine took the layout of a four cylinder engine with parallel cylinders set in a square with wobble-plate drive; the engine was capable of delivering 15hp at 3000rpm (2).

A simplified form of Franchot's engine was, however, used in a very successful engine designed in America by Rider.

Although Ericsson seems not to have undertaken any modification to his caloric engines after 1858, patents for improvements were taken out by Alexander K. Rider of New York. It is interesting to note that his patents were assigned to himself, C. H. Delamater and G. H. Reynolds. Delamater manufactured Ericsson's engines. Two patents were granted to Rider in 1871 for improvements in air engines (US patents 111,087 and 111,088 dated 17.1.1871). In the first patent Rider stated:

'My invention embraces important improvements in that class of air engine described in the patents granted by the United States to John Ericsson, dated July 32, 1855 and December 14, 1858.

In this class of engine, which I will term the aspirating or Ericsson, two pistons are employed in one cylinder, which performs the double office of air pump and power-cylinder.

The objects of my invention – first, to combine this class of

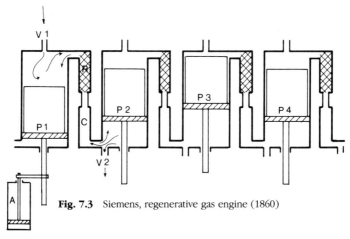

Fig. 7.3 Siemens, regenerative gas engine (1860)

173

aspirating or double piston engine with an internal or closed furnace, in which the air is heated by passing through or over the fire, thereby greatly increasing the power and efficiency of this class of engine as hitherto constructed. Second, to introduce the peculiar motions of the inner or shifting piston by simple, inexpensive, and very efficient mechanism.

Third, to make the engine reversible, so that it may be applied as a transport motor, by means of a mere change of certain parts, with suitable changes of valve motion.

Fourth, to more perfectly regulate the speed of the engine under load without waste of fuel. This is done by peculiar valve and passages arranged to be controlled thereby, the valve being adapted by the governor.'

The second of Rider's patents followed the general lines of Ericsson's 1858 engine but working vertically, not horizontally. In this patent he claimed:

'My invention employs a changing piston, by the aid of which, in connection with a suitable working-piston and valves, and passages, the cold air is received and compressed in the same cylinder which is employed to work off the heated and expanded air.

This mode of operation has been long known, and involves marked advantages, among which is the reduction in cost of the engine from that required when two cylinders, one serving as a pump and the other as a working cylinder, are employed, and an increased degree of coolness, and durability, and facility for lubrication of the parts.

A portion of my invention relates to certain novel means of producing a proper motion of the changer or shifter. Another portion relates to the construction of the furnace and of the adjacent parts where the air is heated by a fire maintained outside of the cylinder and its connected passages. Another portion relates to devices for increasing the power by the aid of a cut-off valve, peculiarly arranged and operated to directly and immediately control the admission of the heated air to the cylinder.'

Rider's modification to the construction of the furnace simplified the construction of the supply cylinder. In order to effect an increase in the heating surface Ericsson had attached a cylindrical skirt to the piston. What Rider did was to remove the skirt from the supply piston and modify the bottom of the cylinder to form a similar shape. The top of the furnace was contoured to follow the cylinder bottom, but leaving a small gap between them. As the supply piston moves, air is passed through the gap becoming heated in the same way as in Ericsson's engine, but the amount of heating surface being swept by the moving air is kept constant, unlike in Ericsson's where it diminished as the supply piston moved on its outward stroke.

A third patent was taken out on the 24th October 1871 (US patent 120325) for what seems to be an engine based on Ericsson's design of 1856, modified for use with an internal furnace. Rider described his improvements as follows:

'My invention relates to provisions for making the cylinder serve as a pump by the aid of the same piston which yields the power; a positive motion of the valve which admits the cold air; a non-conducting lining within the cylinder; a non-conducting lining for the air-pipes and other parts; provisions for heating and re-heating the air in the working cylinder after it has been introduced there-in; provisions for introducing the air into the top of the furnace and taking it out again through the same aperture when the heat is too great; means for arresting the conduction of heat from the hot to the cold end of the cylinder; a peculiar construction and arrangement of the door and means for securing it; an arrangement by which a working beam is employed mounted on a movable link with a parallel motion; and a lining of the entire furnace with firebrick, except a portion of the top, which latter comes under the domed bottom of the working cylinder.

The engine is adapted to stand upright in a small space, and is intended to work rapidly and serve as a quick acting and highly efficient engine for all general purposes – small manufactures, pumping, & co.'

The designs so far discussed may not have been too successful, as Rider went on to design an engine with two loaded pistons. In this design (UK patent 3404, of 1875) the pistons were of equal diameter but of unequal stroke, set to run 90 deg out of phase, as compared with the earlier designs of what were effectively two unequal diameter pistons of equal stroke and 180 deg out of phase. The main component of the new engine, fig. 7.4, were a cold compressing cylinder, C, and a hot power cylinder, D, of longer stroke running some 85-98 deg in advance of the cold cylinder. The two cylinders were connected via regenerator R made up of thin iron plates.

This new design of Rider's was effectively half a Franchot engine. The manufacture of this engine was taken up both in the USA and UK. In America the Delameter Iron Works sold the improved 'Rider Compres-

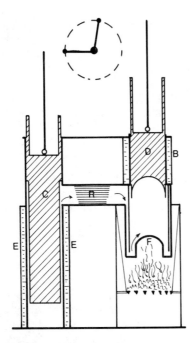

Fig. 7.4 Rider engine

sion (Hot Air) Pumping Engine' in six sizes, 4in, 4·25in, 5in, 6in, 8in and 10in.

The Rider-Ericsson Engine Co., which took over from the Delameter Iron Works and the Rider Engine Co., sold the 'Reeco Rider' engine in four sizes, 5in, 6in, 8in and 10in. The engine was also built by the American Machine Co, who sold the 'Denny' Improved Rider Hot Air Pumping Engine in two sizes, 6in and 8in.

In England the engine was built in three sizes, 5in or 0·25hp, 6·75in or 0·5hp and 10·25in or 1hp sizes, by Hayward-Tyler. The following is taken from a Hayward-Tyler catalogue of about 1912:

DESCRIPTION AND MODE OF WORKING

The 'Rider-Patent' Hot Air Engine, of which we have made many hundreds for pumping purposes, is one of the simplest motors in existence, without valves or small working parts, and is stoked like an ordinary hot-house stove. It is easily understood and managed by gardeners or indoor servants.

The compression piston C first compresses the cold air in the lower part of the compression cylinder A into about one-third its normal volume, when, by the advancing or upward motion of the power piston D, and the completion of the down stroke of the compression piston C, the air is transferred from the compression cylinder A through the regenerator H, and into the heater F, without appreciable change in volume. The result is a greater increase of pressure, corresponding to the increase of temperature, and this impels the power piston up to the end of its stroke. The pressure still remaining in the cylinder and reacting on the compression piston C forces the latter upward till it reaches nearly the top of its stroke, when, by the cooling of the charged air, the pressure falls to its minimum, the power piston descends, and the compression again begins. In the meantime the heated air in passing through the regenerator has left the greater portion of its heat in the regenerator plates to be picked up, and utilised on the return of the air towards the heater. This process re-occurs at each revolution. The lower portion of the compression cylinder A is kept cold by a current of water which circulates through the cooler E, which surrounds the lower portion of the cylinder. In pumping engines the water which is pumped answers this purpose. The heater F should be kept at a dull red heat by a steady fire (of coke generally) which is underneath it.

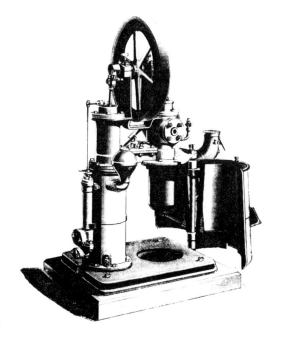

Plate 19 Hayward-Tyler pumping engine

The furnace is of the simplest kind, similar to an ordinary greenhouse stove. There are no valves or stuffing boxes to get out of order. The packings K are simple discs of leather; those on the hot side should be kept cool by the water which circulates round the upper portion of the cylinder at B, so that there is no danger of overheating them.

The same air is used continuously, as there is neither influx or escape, the air being merely shifted from one cylinder to the other.

L is a simple check valve which admits the air when the engine is started, and also supplies any slight leakage which may occur. It is generally placed on the back of the engine, at the lower part of the compression cylinder.

Fig. 7.5 shows the relative phase displacement of the two pistons. The shaded area indicates the change in volume of the air below the two pistons; the expanding air acts on both pistons to a greater or lesser extent depending on the relative position of both pistons.

As heated air is expanded mainly beneath the hot piston there was a need to protect it from damage from overheating, by fitting an extension filled with non-conducting material. The actual heating chamber is an extended surface type as used by Rider in his early designs and devised by Ericsson. The heater was made of cast iron and, it seems, burnt out after a period of use. In early engines they were difficult to replace due to the fact that the engine was partly supported by the furnace, a large portion of which had to be removed before access could be gained to the heater. In 1886 there was patented a modification to the furnace which, it was claimed, greatly simplified the

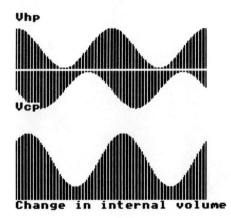

Fig. 7.5 Rider engine phase displacement

job (C. R. Oakes, UK patent 10034). The engine was supported by the cold cylinder and a post to one side of the furnace, and the firebox itself was split into two parts, which bolted up in use, and could be swung apart on hinges when changing the heater. Hayward-Tyler claimed that a new heater could be fitted in two hours with ease.

Rider engines were widely used as pumping engines, the water pump being directly connected to the power piston. However, for deep well pumping the pump was in some designs driven via belting or gears fitted to an extension on a modified crankshaft. Apart from water pumping the quietness of operation proved popular for other uses, as the following letter to the *Musical Times* of 1st July 1879 shows:

> I see in your issue of June 1st a letter entitled 'Gas engines for organs' and as I take great interest in these matters I should like to add to information contained in your correspondent's letter that the large organ in Salisbury Cathedral is blown by a gas engine of Otto's. But for an organ capable of being blown by an engine of 1hp or less, I would like to recommend another form of engine, namely the 'Rider Hot-Air Engine'. I have a small one of ½hp in my house for an eight stop organ, and it answers most admirably.
>
> The makers were good enough at my suggestion to adapt a gas-burner, instead of burning coke; and all I have to do is light it twenty minutes before I require it, and then, without the least trouble it starts to work and continues 2 or 3 hours without attention when it may be necessary to oil the moving parts. Another great advantage consists in the fact that it makes no more noise than a sewing machine. I should add that I burn 25ft of gas per hour which at the high price of gas in this town (5/- per 100) amounts to just 1½d.
>
> Believe me yours faithfully
C. H. Fynes-Clinton.

Blandford Rectory,
Dorset.
June 18 1879.

C. H. Fynes-Clinton was rector of the Church of Peter and Paul, Blandford, from 1877 to 1913. The church was lit by gas in 1840 and electric light was installed in 1920.

For pumping water these engines did, it seems, run successfully for upwards of 30 years with little trouble or maintenance, probably due to the low speed of operation and working pressure of about 20psi. All makers made great play of the engines' simple operation, and Hayward-Tyler gave the following instructions for installation and operation:

GENERAL DIRECTIONS FOR THE FIXING ETC.

Foundation. The engines are attached to a strong cast-iron bed-plate, with holes to receive the holding down bolts. The bed-plate should stand on a foundation of concrete or brickwork; the holding down bolts passing through it. A stone slab between the engine and the concrete is an advantage. A lithographed plan of foundation, to scale, will be sent on application.

Chimney. The chimney need only be 8 feet high, made of ordinary stove pipe. It can be taken through the roof or side of the building or shed in which the engine stands. Should the engine be placed near the chimney of the house this pipe may be carried into the chimney. If the house chimney be tall, leave an opening of about 1½ inches all around the stove pipe where it enters the brick chimney. This is to prevent too great a draught. CARE SHOULD BE TAKEN TO AVOID EXCESSIVE DRAUGHT. In all cases a damper T in the flue is supplied with the engine to regulate the draught as well as the movable damper S under the fire door.

Plunger leathers. The plungers C and D work in leather packings. Those in the collar of the compressing cylinder are not liable to be damaged by overheating; but those in the collar of the power cylinder B must be protected by circulation of water. While the engine is running the water circulates through this collar, but when the engine is to be stopped it is desirable to let it run down and cool as much as possible so that it stops of itself, then fill the small hollow around the collar of the cylinder B adjoining the plungers with cold water, to keep the leathers soft. THIS PROVISION IS IMPORTANT. For further protection of the leathers a small circulating tank may be used, water from which is turned on when the water ceases pumping.

Lubrication. Before starting the engine, the glass lubricators on the main bearings N N should be removed and a few drops of oil poured into the holes. The glass lubricators should be filled up and put back into their places. The small brass cups on the ends of the connecting rods O O should also be filled with oil, also the cups P for oiling the bottom ends of the connecting rods. Ordinary machine oil of good quality should be used. The leather packings in which the plungers work should also be lubricated before starting the engine and at about three hours interval whilst working with a small quantity of the LUBRICATING CREAM WE SUPPLY IN TINS, or if this is not available with paraffin oil of the best quality. Take care not to oil too freely.

Management of the fire. Ordinary gas coke broken up into pieces about the size of a large walnut is the best fuel, as it makes no smoke. Hard wood is a very good fuel. A FIERCE FIRE IS NOT REQUISITE but should be fed at regular intervals. The heater F should never be allowed to become white hot – a red glow is sufficient. This can easily be regulated by the damper T in the flue pipe elbow, and by removable damper S in under the fire door.

Starting the engine. The fire should be lighted half-an-hour before it is required to start the engine. When the lower cylinder or the part marked B is beginning to get hot, and the heater red as seen through the inspection hole W, the engine is ready for starting. The small cock on the top of the regenerator H should be closed and the flywheel pulled over one or two revolutions, the direction being as shown by the arrow; the engine will then start. The easiest plan to start the engine is to first swing the flywheel to and fro before turning it round, making use of the momentum to compress the air which is drawn in through the sucking valve or check valve L on the bed-plate.

Working. When once the engine is started no attention is necessary beyond regulating the fire and lubricating the bearings and plungers (see 'lubrication'). THE DAMPERS UNDER THE FIRE DOOR SHOULD ALWAYS BE LEFT CLOSED AFTER THE ENGINE IS FULLY STARTED.

Stopping the engine. It is desirable to let the engine run down, and cool as much as possible, so that it stops itself, but to stop it, it is only necessary to open the small cock M on the regenerator. When the engine is stopped, the fire should always be raked out, the fire door left open, also the damper in the flue and some water placed in the hollow round plunger D.

Letting out water to prevent freezing. A cock Q is provided at bottom of cooler for drawing off water from cooling chamber E in frosty weather. THIS IS NECESSARY TO PREVENT BURSTING THE WATER JACKET by frost.

Blowing out cock. The cock R is for blowing out waste oil when necessary. This should be partially opened once or twice a week when the engine is running.

THESE ENGINES WORK WITHOUT EXPLOSION.

The mention that the engine worked without explosion was to distinguish them from the internal combustion engines then coming into general use. The lubricating cream was sold in 2lb tins at 6/6d each.

Rider used in his engine a regenerator made up of 24 thin cast iron plates set ⅟₃₂in apart and placed sideways in the air passage between the hot and cold cylinders. By experiment the efficiency was found to be 60% (3).

In 1896 a Rider engine was tested by the Massachusetts Institute of Boston (4). The engine used had a hot piston of 6·7in in diameter with a 9·5in stroke; the cold piston was 6·75in in diameter with an 8·6in stroke. The test results were:

RPM	IHP	BHP	Mechanical efficiency, %
138	0·81	0·23	29
128	0·66	0·23	35
118	0·58	0·19	33
128	0·66	0·26	42
143	0·78	0·30	38
136	0·68	0·29	43
75	0·45	0·18	39

For their size Rider engines gave very little power, mainly due to the slow running speed.

Fig. 7.6 shows indicator diagrams taken in 1881 from an engine with 210mm dia pistons, hot piston stroke of 292mm and cold piston stroke of 265mm (5, 6). A is the diagram from the hot cylinder and B from the cold or compressing cylinder.

To give some idea of the sizes of these engines the following tables have been compiled from various makers' price lists.

Rider-Ericsson Engine Co. 1906

Dia of cylinders in	Ht to top of flywheel ft in	Floor space ft in × ft in	Approximate weight in lb	RPM
5	5 0	2 2 × 2 9	1250	120-160
6	6 0	2 4 × 3 4	2000	100-120
8	7 2	2 5 × 3 11	3200	100-120
10	7 9	2 8 × 4 4	3700	80-110

The price for the basic machine was from $210 for the 5-in engine to $540 for the 10-in engine.

Hayward-Tyler 1912

Dia of cylinders in	Length of stroke in	Ht to top of flywheel ft in	Floor space ft in × ft in	Approx. weight	RPM
5	6·25	4 10	2 2 × 3 0	10cwt 3qr	140
6·75	9·5	5 9	2 2 × 3 6	18cwt 3qr	120
10·25	13	7 6	2 8 × 5 0	36cwt	100

Engine size	Delivery with 2in pump gal/hr	Height of delivery feet	Price with 2in pump
No. 1 (·25hp)	500	40	£42
No. 2 (·5hp)	600	70	£51
No. 3 (1hp)	680	125	£86

It is interesting to note that Rider designed a flame ignition gas engine based on the layout of his hot air engine (UK patent 2129, 1879).

Several modifications were made to Rider's hot air engine by Alexander Monski of Eilburg, Germany. In his first patent Monski describes a double-acting Rider engine (DRP.20053, 1882). The engine consisted of three cylinders, two hot and one cold. The cold cylinder contained a double acting piston, which was connected via air passages

Fig. 7.6 Rider engine indicator diagram

to the two hot cylinders built as in a normal Rider engine, one hot cylinder being connected below the cold piston, the other above. The hot pistons were connected to cranks set 180 deg apart with the cold piston half-way between the two.

In his second patent Monski details improvements in heating and cooling the air (DRP.34493, 1885) and his third (DRP.34542, 1885) was for improvements in the regenerator.

As in most things there was a second-hand market for hot air engines and the following adverts for Rider engines were found in the pages of the *English Mechanic and World of Science* (for the years 1880-1881).

A BARGAIN. – FOR SALE, one-horse power HOT AIR ENGINE (Riders patent), by Hayward Tyler and Co; combined for power and pumping, in splendid condition; only been worked for a few months; cost £94, want £60 for it. – N. S. Reiley, Shelton House, Littlehampton.

HALF-HORSE RIDER HOT-AIR PUMPING-ENGINE for sale, nearly new, and in perfect order; removed only to make way for a larger engine; has raised all the water for a large house for six months; about 800 gallons raised 54 feet in one hour forty minutes. Very simple and economical; has pulley for driving, and governor, and was used to drive a very heavy lathe. Cost nearly £60; price £35. – Address, H. Mullens, Emberfield, Hampton Wick.

1/4 HP Rider Hot-Air-Engine, nearly new, for sale cheap, only been used a few times – MILLER and TUPP, Steam Launch builders, Creek Works, Middle Mail, Hammersmith, London.

References

Chapter One

(1) The Pneumatics of Heron of Alexandria. Edited by Bennit Woodcroft. 1851.
(2) Marcus Vitruvius – De Architecture. Book 1. ch 11. Edited by Frank Granger. The Loeb Classical Library. 1970.
(3) I tre libre de spiritali, cioe dinalfar acque per forze dell'aria. Giovanni Battista della Porta. Naples, 1606.
(4) Les raisons des forces mouvantes avec diverses machines et pluisieurs dessins de grottes et de fontaines. Isaac de Caus. 1615.
(5) Translated into English by John Leak in 1659. 'New and useful inventions for water works: a work both useful and delightful for all sorts of people.'
(6) Magic Natural. Giovanni Battista Della Porta. 1558. Three books enlarged in 1589 to twenty books.
(7) Mysteryes of Nature and Art, The first on water works, the second on Fyer works, the third of Drawing, Colouring, Painting. J. Bate. London, 1634.
(8) The Art of Drawing Water. Robert D'Acres. London, 1659. Reprinted in 1930 by the Newcomen Society.
(9) Method of substituting the force of fire for horse and man power to move machines. G. Amontons. Memoirs de l'Academie des Sciences. 1699.
(10) Nicolsons Journal. Vol 29. 1811. Pages 175-177.
(11) Sadi Carnot and the Cagnard Engine. T. S. Kuhn. ISES. Vol 52. 1961. Pages 567-574.
(12) Proceedings of the Institute of Civil Engineers. Vol 9. Page 199.
(13) J. A. Chaldecott, Ann Sci, 1952. Vol 8. Pages 195-201.
(14) Commentaria in primam fen primi libri Canonis Avicennae. Santoria Santorii. Venetijis, 1625.
(15) Meteorologica Cosmica. Frankfurt. 1626. Philosophica Moysaica. Gouda. 1638. Utriusqui Cosmi Historia. Oppenheim. 1617.
(16) Ottomic de Guericke. Experimenta nove (ut vacanturi) . . . Amsterdam. 1672.
(17) A. G. Thoday. Barometers, HMSO.
(18) Liquid Piston Stirling Engines. C. D. West. New York. 1983.

Chapter Two

(1))Aristotle on the Heavens. The Loeb Classical Library.

(2) Marcus Vitruvius – De Architecture. Book 5, ch 10. The Loeb Classical Library (Heineman). 1970.

(3))Environmental Conditions in Coal Mines. John Sinclair. London. 1958.

(4) Cyclopaedia of Arts, Science and Literature. Abraham Rees. London. 1819. (Subject air pipes.)

(5) Natural Philosophy. A. Privart Deschanel. London. 1885. Pages 308-309.

(6))Lighting by Gas. Dean Chandler. Metropolitan Gas Co. London. 1936.

(7) Imperial Journal of Science. Manchester (1880?). Vol 3. Pages 37-40.

(8) Electrical Review. 11/2/1983.

(9) Science and Civilisation in China. John Needham. Cambridge. 1962. Vol 4. Pages 123-125.

(10) Medieval Technology and Social Change. Lynn White. Oxford. 1962. Page 116.

(11) Leonardo da Vinci. Codex Atlanticus folio 5. Ambrosiam Library, Milan.

(12) De Varient. J. Carden. Rerum libre (XII) C.58. 1548.

(13) Mathematical Magic. John Wilkins. London. 1648.

(14) Maestro dell Art dell Curcina. Barttolomeo Scappi. Rome. 1572. Reprinted in Venice in 1622

(15) Travel Journal. Michel Montaigne. 1581.

(16) Novo Teatro di Machine. Vittoria Zonca. Padua. 1607. (Published after his death in 1602.)

(17) Lc Machine. Giovanne Branca. Rome. 1629.

(18) Electrical Review. 5th June 1981. Vol 208, no. 21. 16th April 1982. Vol 210, no. 15.

(19) De Celo & Mundo. Albert Magnus. Venetijs. 1495.

(20) Metrologum de Pisce Cane et Volucre. Giovanni da Fontana. Bologna. (Biblioteca Universitaria MS 2705 ff 95^v-104^v.)

(21) A History of Flying. C. H. Gibbs Smith. London. 1953.

(22) Ibid 4, subject – Aerostation.

(23) Zanussi Transatlantic Balloon. C. Davy and D. Cameron. Jersey. 1982.

(24) How To Make and Fly Model Hot Air Balloons. Ray Morse. London. 1978.

Chapter Three

(1) The Steam Engine of Thomas Newcomen. L. Rolt and J. Allen. Moorland Publishing Co. 1977. Pages 147-148.

(2) The Engineer. 13th August 1948. Pages 168-169.

(3) Reprinted in 1960 with the posthumous papers on the second law of thermodynamics by E. Chapeyion and R. Clousius. Reflections on the motive power of heat – Sadi Carnot. Edited by E. Mendza. Dover Publications. New York. 1960.

Chapter Four

(1) Nicolsons Journal. Vol 18. 1807. Pages 260-262.

(2) Use of Heat as a motive power. B. Cheverton. Proc. I.C.E., 1853.

(3) Sir George Cayley. J. Laurance Pritchard. London. 1961.

(4) Steam on Common Roads. William Fletcher. London. 1891.

Plate 20   Furnace gas engine

(5) Scientific American. 14/2/1883.
(6) Engineering. 20/4/1883.
(7) Gas Oil and Air Engines. B. Donkin. London. 1911.
(8) Engineering. 14/1/1887.
(9) Electric Light for Lighthouses. Proc. I.C.E. Vol LVII. 1878.
(10) Engineer. 1/6/1867. Pages 510-511.
(11) Engineering. 10/1/1868 and 13/3/1868.
(12) Wenham's Heated Air Engine. Proceedings Of Institute of Mechanical Engineers. 1873.
(13) The Howard superheated Air Engine. Engineering. 24/1/1873. Pages 68-69.
(14) Engineering. 30/8/1889.
(15) De Kraftmachine des Kleinewerbs. J. O. Kroke. Berlin. 1899.
(16) Ibid 7
(17) Brayton Hydro Carbon Oil Engine. The Engineer. 18/7/1878.

(18) Internal Fire. C. Lyle Cummings. Oregon. 1976.
(19) The Gas Petrol and OIl Engine. Dugald Clerk. London. 1910.
(20) The Book of Modern Engines. Rankin Kennedy. London. 1912.
(21) Elements of Physics. Neil Arnott. 1833.
(22) The Gas Turbine. Henry H. Supple. London. 1910.

Chapter Five

(1) For some reason, not definitely ascertained, Stirling's patent does not appear in the Blue Book series. A manuscript copy of his Scottish patent was produced in the case of Neilson v. Baired in 1843. This was reproduced in the Journal of the Iron and Steel Institute in 1886 (pages 831 to 838).

A copy of Stirling's English patent was found in 1917 and was reproduced in *The Engineer* on 14th December 1917 (pages 516 to 517). An extract of the patent also appeared in the Proceedings of the Institute of Civil Engineers for 1853, in a paper 'Heated Air Engines' by James Leslie.
(2) British Library. Woodcroft collection, M. S. Stirling.
(3) Proceedings of Institute of Civil Engineers Vol No. 44.
(4) Description of Stirling's improved Air Engine – James Stirling.
Proceedings of Institute of Civil Engineers. Vol 4. 1845.
(5) Stirling's Air Engine – Patrick Stirling. The Engineer. 8th February 1861.
(6) Account of Stirling's Air Engine – Patrick Stirling. Transactions of the Institute of Engineers in Scotland. Vol. 4..
(7) Air Engines. Engineering. 1875.
(8) Tresca.
Sur une machine a air chaud de Laubereau. Ann du Conns Imp des Arts et metiers. Paris. 4ᵉ année. Page 113.
(9) Delba.
Die Laubereau-Schwartzkopt'sche Heissluftmaschine. Dingler's Poly Journal. 1864. Pages 81-108.
(10) Eckerth.
Versuche uber Lemann'sche Heissluftmaschine. Technischen Blattern. Prague. 1869. Page 104.
(11) Delba.
Mitteilungen uber neuesten Fortschritte bezuglich der Dampf-, Gas und Heissluftmaschinen. Dingler's Poly Journal. 194. 1869. Pages 157-176.
(12) Proc. I.E.E. Vol 121. No. 7. July 1974. Pages 649-751.
(13) Electrical Review. Vol 210. No. 17. April 1982. Page 19.
(14) The Mechanical Production of Gold. J.A. Ewing. Cambridge. 1923.
(15) The Mechanical Production of Gold. Minutes Proc. I.C.E. Vol 37.
(16) Phillips Tech. Review. Fundamentals of the Gas Refrigerating Machine. J. W. Kohler. Vol 16. No. 3. Pages 69-78. 1954.
Construction of Gas Refrigerating Machines. Vol 16. No. 4. Pages 105-115. 1954.

Chapter Six

(1))A Description of a new method of employing the combustion of fuel as a moving power.
Paper No. 119 Institute of Civil Engineers, 1827.
(2) Life of John Ericsson. W. C. Church. Sampson Low. London. 1890.

(3) Elements of Physics or Natural Philosophy. Neil Arnott. London. 1833.
(4) Mechanics Magazine. London. 9/11/1833.
(5) Proceedings of the Institute of Mechanical Engineers. Page 79. 1873.
(6) Contributions to the Centennial Exhibition. John Ericsson. 1876.
(7) Scientific American. Page 149. New York. 22/1/1853.
(8) New York Daily Times. 12/1/1853.
(9) Ibid 7.
(10) John Ericsson and the Age of the Caloric. Eugene S. Fergusson. Bulletin 228. Smithsonian Institution. 1961.
(11) Ericsson's Caloric Engine. Articles taken from the daily journals of the City of New York. Washington. 1853. Page 6.
(12) Ibid 8.
(13) National Intelligencer. Washington. 25th February and 3rd March 1853.
(14) American Journal of Science and Arts (Sillmans Journal of Science). Ser. 2 Vol 15. Pages 384-395. 1853.
(15) Ibid 8.
(16) Appleton's Mechanics Magazine and Engineers Journal. Drawing of engine is shown in Plate 3. Pages 82-86, 152-158, 217-221. Vol 3. February 1853.
(17) (a) Appleton's Mechanics Magazine 1853. 262hp.
     (b) Scientific American 1853. 244·572hp
     (c) Mechanics Magazine (London) Vol 58. 208hp
     (d) American Journal of Science 1853. 316hp
     (e) Proceedings of the American Academy of Arts and Science, Vol 3. 116hp
     (f) Proceedings of the Institute of Civil Engineers, 1853. 208hp and 226hp.
(18) Steam, Air and Gas Engines. John Bourn. London.
(19) Ibid 6. Page 443.
(20) The Engineer. 15/4/1881. Page 273. London.

Chapter Seven

(1) G. H. Babcock. Substitutes for Steam. ASME Transactions. Vol VII. 1885-1886.
(2) The Construction of the Philips Air Engine. Philips Technical Review. Vol 9. No. 5. 1947.
(3) Kraftmaschinen de Kleinenwerbes. J. O. Knoke. Page 131.
(4) Techy Quarterly. 1898. USA.
(5) Uber Die Heissluftmaschine von Rider. R. Schottler. Zeitschrift des Vereines Deutscher Ingenieure. Vol 25. 1881.
(6) Ibid 3. Page 123.

Index — Names

Plate 21   Stolze hot air turbine

Index — Subjects

By fire:
Robert D'Acres, 15
Bewley & Holtham, 50
Samuel Brown, 26
Harwell, 25
P. A. Kuhne, 29
Montgolfier & Dayme, 23

Smoke Jacks
Horse-riding lamp, 36

For cooking:
John Braithwait, 41
Jerome Carden, 37
Barttolmea Scappi, 39

Samuel Pepys, 40
John Prosser, 40
John Thin, 41
Vittoria Zonca, 39
Leonardo da Vinci, 37

Driving machinery:
Giovanne Branca, 39
Joseph Haterly, 41
John Payn, 41

Solar Chimney:
Isidora Cabanyes, 41
Manzanares, 42

Index — Illustrations

Plates

Line diagrams

196

OTHER ENGINEERING TITLES IN THE ARGUS BOOKS RANGE

Hardening, Tempering and Heat Treatment
Vertical Milling in the Home Workshop
Screwcutting in the Lathe
Foundrywork for the Amateur
Milling Operations in the Lathe
Measuring and Marking Metals
Art of Welding
Sheet Metal Work
Soldering and Brazing
Saws and Sawing
Electroplating
Drills, Taps and Dies
The Amateur's Lathe
Book of the Unimat
Myford Series 7 Lathe Manual
Projects for the Unimat
Using the Small Lathe
The Amateur's Workshop
Building the Universal Pillar Tool
Dividing and Graduating
Model Engineer's Handbook (2nd Ed)
The 'Quorn': Universal Tool and Cutter Grinder
Simple Workshop Devices
Model Four-stroke Petrol Engines
The Model Steam Locomotive
Introducing Model Traction Engine Construction

plus books on individual models of locomotives, traction and stationary engines etc. and model aircraft, boats and cars

Argus Books
1 Golden Square, London W1R 3AB

send s.a.e. for latest book list